home
screen
printing
workshop

QUARRY

home
screen
printing
workshop

GLOUCESTER MASSACHUSETTS

QUARRY BOOKS

Do-it-Yourself Techniques, Design Ideas, and Tips for Graphic Prints

PAUL THIMOU

First published in the United States of America by
Quarry Books, a member of
Quayside Publishing Group
33 Commercial Street
Gloucester, Massachusetts 01930-5089
Telephone: (978) 282-9590
Fax: (978) 283-2742
www.rockpub.com

Library of Congress Cataloging-in-Publication Data
Thimou, Paul.
    Home screen printing workshop : do-it-yourself techniques, design ideas, and tips for graphic prints / Paul Thimou.
        p.   cm.
    ISBN 1-59253-271-3 (pbk.)
    1. Screen process printing. I. Title.
    TT273.T55 2006
    746.6'2—dc22   2006014528
                                                                               CIP

ISBN-13: 978-1-59253-271-1
ISBN-10: 1-59253-271-3

10 9 8 7 6 5 4 3 2 1

Design: Richard Oriolo
Manuscript Editor: Shannon Howard

Printed in Singapore

Contents

SECTION 1
Basic Printing Methods

SECTION 2
Special Topics

Introduction

Images produced by the process of screen printing surround us everywhere we go. They can be found on the garments we wear, the pillows we lay our heads on, the bags we carry our belongings in, and the mugs that hold our coffee in the morning. Because the need to personalize our belongings and decorate our environment is so powerful, we go to tremendous lengths to set ourselves apart and herald our individuality, often spending a lot of time and money finding and buying things that express who we are. But purchasing unique objects, especially those that are not mass produced, can be a real challenge—unless we create them. That's where screen printing comes in.

Screen printing allows for easy and fast printing of an image, to create a repeated design or a number of separate prints. Once an image is made into a screen, it can be printed on a variety of surfaces such as cloth, paper, leather, wood, and even glass. By using different printing techniques, the same image can appear on a surface in different colors or with a different look. And by using a different screen for each color of a design, multiple-color designs can also be produced.

On the following pages, the screen printing process will be described in detail. Methods of making screens will be analyzed. Printing techniques and image manipulation will be discussed to help you achieve the best results possible every time you print. The more methods of expression you know, the better you'll be able to make a bold visual statement.

This book aims to simplify screen printing in a way that can be used by artists and craftspeople in many environments. Screen printing can be done on almost any table anywhere—in the garage, basement, studio, or even the kitchen. (That's how Laura Ashley started her design empire in London.) Whether you're making a T-shirt, tote bag, poster, banner, or fine art print, it can be done for both pleasure and profit, and the process is like taking a fabulous trip to unknown lands. Adventure is waiting for you every time you pull the squeegee, so start printing and have a wonderful journey!

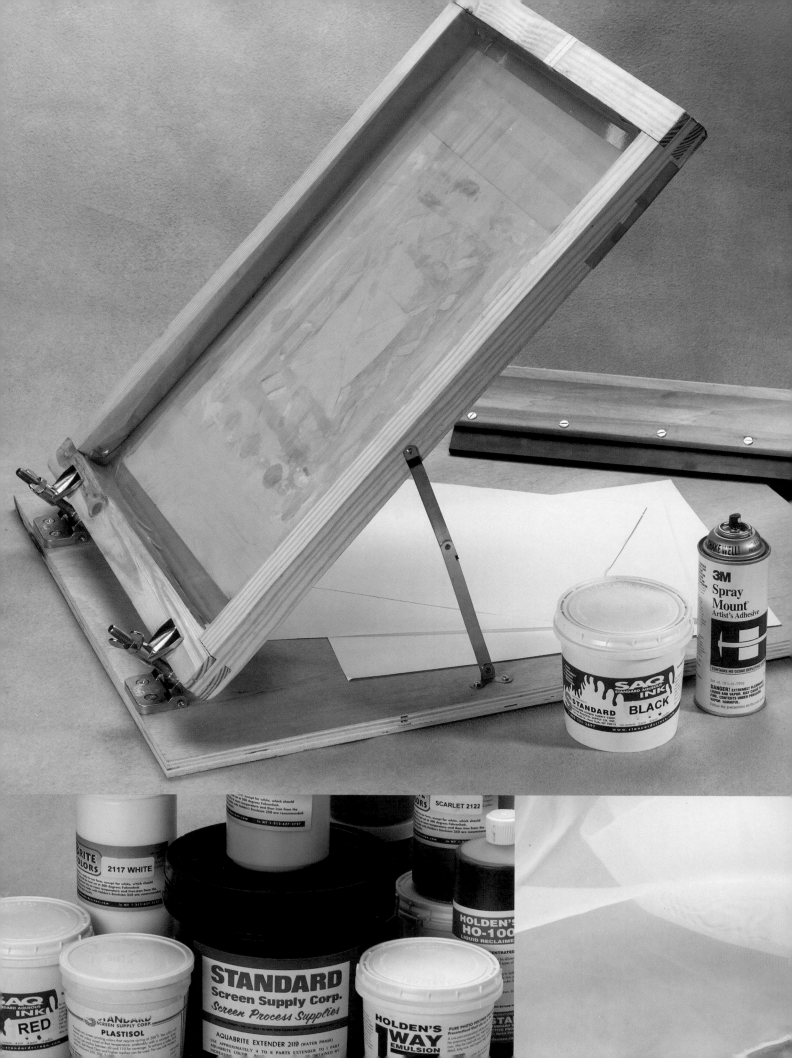

How to Set Up a Small Screen Printing Studio

It's easy to set up a studio for home screen printing. Mainly, you need a long table and some storage space or shelving for inks, screens, squeegees, emulsions, and other supplies. If possible, your work area should have easy access to a sink or wash basin as well as good light and proper air circulation. It should also be situated well away from children, pets, food, and fire sources.

This chapter will explain how to buy or build a work table and will detail the other materials you will need. Once you have the basics in place, you can print to your heart's content!

Printing Equipment

THE TABLE

First, you will need to buy or build a long, flat table. Place it in the center of the space if possible, since you'll want to have access from all sides. Secure the table so it doesn't shake or wobble, and then pad the top with a couple of layers of felt. If you cannot find thick felt, use old blankets. You want to create a medium-soft surface on which your printing will be done. Finish the printing table by covering it with thin (#12) canvas. Make sure both the felt and the canvas are secured by stapling them around the edge of the table. A piece of medium plywood can be placed on the table when a harder surface is needed for tracing, drawing, cutting, pasting, or printing on paper.

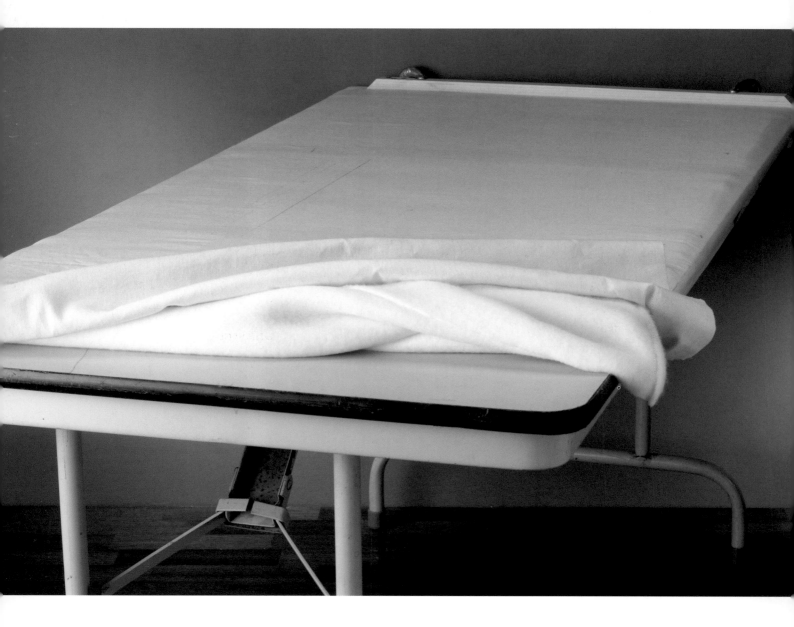

THE PRINTING STATION

A one-person printing station can be purchased at a local screen printing supplier. They come in many styles and price ranges, or one can be made easily by using a $^1/_2$" (1.3 cm) -thick piece of plywood, a pair of hinge clamps, and a sea jay kick leg, all available from a screen print supplier or hardware store.

THE EXPOSURE UNIT

When screens are made photographically, an exposure unit is needed. Exposure units can be purchased, but they also can be improvised easily. Any light source (including the sun) can be used to photograph or "burn" a screen. A wooden box—the size depends on the size of screens used—can be used to make your own exposure unit. After building or buying the box, place several ultraviolet-rich black lights in the bottom. If black lights are not available, any other light source containing UV rays will do. A power switch and a timer will complete the electric connections of the unit, while a piece of glass placed on the top makes it fully functional. The glass should be thick enough to support the screen, as well as the weights used to achieve good contact between the artwork being photographed and the mesh of the screen.

There are two methods of making a stencil in screen printing: direct and indirect. The indirect stencil is done on a separate surface such as film or paper and then is adhered to the mesh of the screen. With the direct method, the stencil is created directly on the mesh of the screen. This is usually done by applying a light-sensitive emulsion to the mesh. Once it is dry, the sensitized mesh is exposed (photographed) to light (see Project 5, page 60).

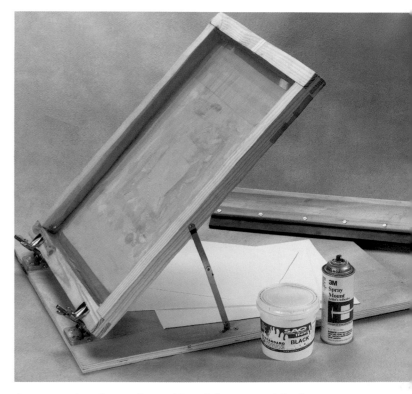

A one-person station can be used for printing on a variety of substrates. Using an adhesive, such as spray mount, will prevent the substrate from moving while you print.

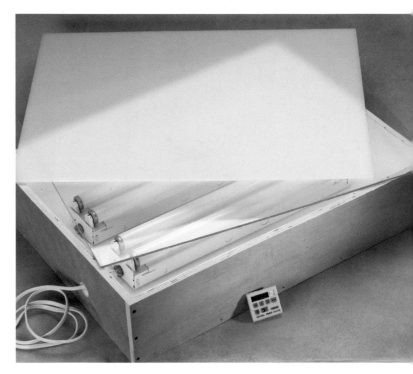

An exposure unit can easily be turned into a light table by placing a frosted piece of acetate on top of the glass. Such a table comes handy when checking positives for opaqueness, repeats, and accurate registrations, or for making simple tracings of artwork.

Basic Supplies

FRAMES

To avoid warping, frames can be made of good-quality kiln-dried wood or aluminum. Aluminum frames are best since they're strong and lightweight, but they require a special stretching table and

Frames come in different sizes and should be made of either wood or aluminum.

Mesh is bought by the roll or by the yard. The I.D. number is printed on the selvage, revealing the number of the mesh. A three-digit number indicates monofilament and a number followed by XX indicates multifilament mesh. The higher the number, the finer the mesh. Mesh comes in three colors: white, yellow, and orange (not shown), each of which has a different effect on the diffraction of light during exposure.

heavy-duty glue to create. An easy way to make a frame is to use canvas stretchers, which are sold in all art supply stores. Such a screen is very shallow and not very strong, but it will do in a pinch.

The size of a screen is measured either as the inner dimension (I.D.) or the outer dimension (O.D.). The inner dimension excludes the frame; the outer includes it. This is important to consider when building the printing table and the exposure unit.

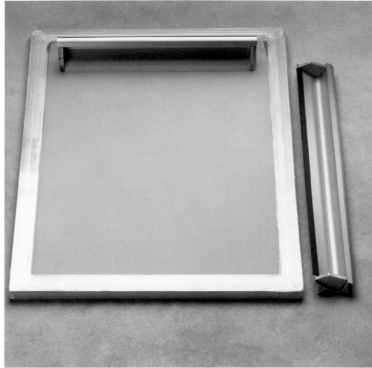

The tool used to apply emulsion onto the screen is called a scoop coater. Scoop coaters come in different sizes. The correct one to use is smaller in size than the frame and larger than the design or printing area.

The artwork, or positive, must be small enough so there is a negative space left around it in the screen in which to put the ink and rest the squeegee during printing. This negative space is referred to as the inkwell.

The frame of this screen was made by using canvas stretchers. This positive is too large for the size of the screen.

MESH

Mesh is the fine fabric we stretch on a frame to create a stencil. Once made from silk (hence the term "silk screen"), it's now almost always made from synthetic fibers such as polyester or nylon. Mesh can be bought by unit of length and is identified according to the fiber used, the openings per square inch, and the kind of thread used. Either monofilament (single thread) or multifilament (many threads twisted together) yarns are used to weave the mesh. The weave determines the number of openings per square inch that will allow the ink to pass through the mesh during the printing process.

The identification number for the mesh describes the properties of the mesh. The higher the number, the finer the mesh. For example, a 300 mesh is much finer than a 120 mesh. Because it has approximately 300 tiny openings per square inch, it allows a very thin layer of ink to pass onto the substrate (or surface being printed), resulting in a finer, more detailed image. This is a desirable size if the substrate is something fine (such as silk or paper) and the image has fine details. But it would be a nightmare trying to print on a T-shirt using metallic ink and a screen with 300 mesh. A much better

The mesh is stretched taut and stapled to the frame. Measuring 8" x 24" (20 x 60 cm) in size (I.D.), these screens are stretched with 110 monofilament mesh and are ready to be used.

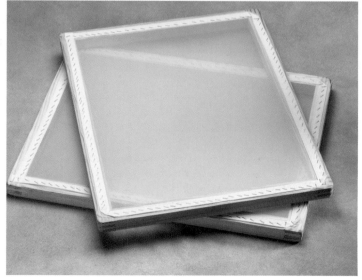

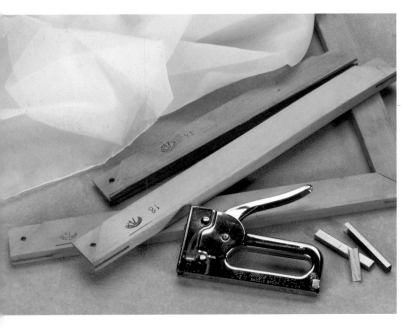

Canvas stretchers make quick and easy print-making frames.

choice would be 80 or 90 mesh, depending on the design and viscosity of the ink.

Besides the commonly used white mesh, yellow and orange are also available. The color helps control the diffraction (scattering) of light during exposure time. Reflecting light from the mesh will contribute to the loss of definition of the image, with orange mesh providing a better resolution than white. Choosing the correct mesh for the job at

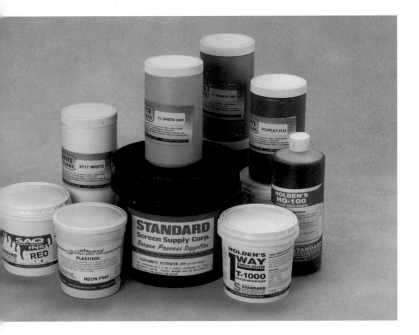

Screen printing inks come in many varieties, including water-based, oil-based, and oil-in-water.

hand will always produce satisfying results and make printing easy and fun.

INKS

There are as many varieties of inks and paints as there are surfaces to print on, but the most commonly used screen printing inks include water-based, oil-based, and oil-in-water. All of these are pigments, which means they sit on the surface of the substrate.

In addition to pigments, dyes can also be used to print on textiles. Dyes must have an affinity for the fiber of the textile being printed or the color will wash off. Unlike pigments, they do not sit on the surface but instead penetrate and bind with the fiber, leaving a softness to the touch. In fact, there is nothing more pleasant to the eye and the hand than dye-printed silk!

Dyes are always transparent, while pigments can be either transparent or opaque. Because transparent inks allow you to see through them, the color of the substrate will affect the final color of the print. Transparent inks can be trapped or layered while printing so that a third color can be produced from the two. For example, if blue is printed first and then a second screen is added with yellow, the overlapping areas will be green.

Transparent inks do not print well on dark substrates. In this case we use opaque inks. Opaque inks, especially plastisol (oil-based ink), look brilliant on black and other dark color substrates. These inks are mixed and ready to be used in many colors. They can also be mixed with each other for a larger variety of tints, shades, and chromas.

You can mix your own colors if you have the time and space. Water-based inks are made with two parts: the colorant (pigment) and the base, which is also referred to as the vehicle or extender. The base, which is made by mixing an extender with a binder, contains all the catalysts needed to make the colorant adhere to the substrate. The base and colorant are mixed together in a proportion of approximately 80–85 percent base to 15–20 percent colorant. They cannot be used separately because the colorant alone would peel off the substrate, and the base by itself is colorless. However, the base by itself can be used to change the substrate.

When printing on textiles, either with pigments or dyes, the print has to be cured or fixed so it becomes washable. This is done either by steam (for some dyes) or heat (for some pigments). If heat is required for the fixing, you can slowly pass a hot iron over the back of the printed area, or place a clean cloth between the iron and the print to avoid scorching.

Not all inks require heat to become cured and washable. Some only require a certain amount of exposure to air. Usually the manufacturer will inform the consumer of the proper method.

Manufacturers of all chemicals used in the process of screen printing are required by law to make material safety data sheets (MSDS) available to consumers. For every chemical used in your studio, you must have its MSDS. This is very important information that must be read and followed for good health and a safer work environment.

SUBSTRATES

The surface being printed upon is referred to as the substrate. The substrate can be anything from cloth to wood, or any other surface, but it's important to remember that the color and texture of the substrate will affect the final print. During printing, the substrate must be stretched and held taut under the screen. This can be achieved by pinning it with T-pins or laying it on a surface that has been covered with a thin layer of specially made glue. In some instances, vacuum tables that keep the substrate flat and in place are used.

The quality and composition of the substrate are important elements to consider when choosing the size of the mesh, the durometer and profile of the squeegee, the ink, and the number of passes needed. A substrate with a finished surface, such as

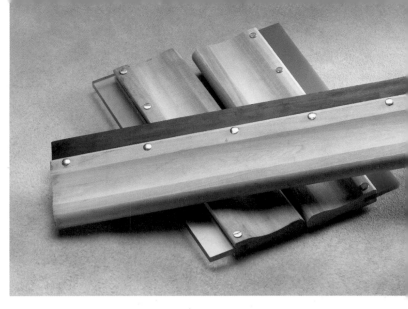

Squeegees come in different sizes and are sold by the inch. They are available with polyurethane blades, which are firm and solvent resistant. Other kinds include rubber blades, which are usually black, and Neoprene, which is usually black or gray.

water-resistant fabric, may react with the ink, causing it to run and creating an unwanted shadow effect. It can be an interesting look, but if it's not what you wanted, you'll probably be disappointed. Because it's impossible to detect such a problem prior to printing, you should always prewash all fabrics and test whatever substrate you're using. Testing substrates and the way they react to different pigments is a must in a screen printing studio.

SQUEEGEE

The squeegee is to the printer what the brush is to the painter. It is the tool that pushes the ink through the stencil onto the substrate, and it's what controls the amount of ink passing onto the printing surface. For uniformity of color and easy printing, a squeegee must be larger than the printing area by 3" to 4" (7.5 to 10 cm), so the whole area is printed with one pass.

Squeegees come in different durometers, or degrees of softness. A low (50–60) durometer squeegee is very soft and is used when the substrate requires a large amount of ink. A medium (60–70) durometer squeegee has a blade that is neither soft nor hard. Finally, a high durometer (70–80) squeegee has a very hard blade that allows much less ink to pass through while printing. Therefore, a hard blade is ideal when printing a detailed design on a fine surface such as silk or paper.

A squeegee is also identified by its profile, or the way the blade ends. Round-profile squeegees are best for printing on heavy textiles. If less ink is needed, a square-profile squeegee will be better. And when printing on paper or other fine substrates, a squeegee with a pointy profile will be the best.

The durometer and profile of the squeegee are two of the five ways a squeegee can be manipulated to achieve desirable results. Other ways are:

- **The pressure you physically apply while printing.**

- **The number of passes, or how many times the ink is pressed over the printing area.**

- **The way the squeegee is held while printing. (The greater the angle, the more ink will pass through.)**

PHOTO EMULSION

Any area where the ink does not go through during printing is called a negative area. The surrounding open and therefore printing areas are positives. This is a stencil; it is the basic concept of screen printing.

When a stencil is made photographically, a light-sensitive emulsion is needed. Emulsions are available in two parts. The first part is the base. The second part is the light-sensitive chemical—usually ammonium biochromate or diazo, available either in liquid or powder form. When the base and the chemicals are mixed, they create a light-sensitive emulsion that can be used to transfer an image to a screen.

Emulsions are available in different colors (yellow, green, purple), depending on the manufacturer and the light-sensitive chemical used. Some react faster to light than others. T-1000, a pre-mixed diazo emulsion, is dark green and comes ready to use. A fast emulsion, its exposure time varies from fifteen seconds to two minutes, depending on the transparency of the positive, the opaqueness of the

image, and the light source. Screens can be coated with this solution, stored in a dark, cool place, and used as needed.

Because emulsions become light sensitive after they dry and water insoluble once exposed to light, it's best to apply them in a dimly lit room or a dark-room with a yellow safety light. When coating a screen with emulsion, use a scoop coater. This tool allows a thin layer of emulsion to cover the mesh where the image is going to be photographed. Scoop coaters come in different sizes. Choose one that is smaller than the inner dimension (I.D.) of the frame and larger than the image being photographed.

The best stencil for screen printing, as far as durability and good image resolution goes, is a direct stencil done photographically on the mesh of the screen (see project 3, page 40), but you can also use an indirect or capillary stencil. With this method, the light-sensitive emulsion is spread thinly on a substrate such as film. The film is then exposed to the light with the artwork or image to be printed in between the light source and the sensitized film. Finally, the film is developed in a tray.

During development, the printable areas of the design will dissolve and open up as a stencil, and that stencil will be adhered to the mesh. The undeveloped emulsion fills the mesh, and the base—either film or paper—gets peeled off.

Once a photo stencil has been printed, the mesh can be reused by washing the fixed emulsion off the mesh. While wearing gloves, apply reclaiming liquid (available from any printing supply shop) with a sponge or brush on the printing side of the screen and leave it for a few minutes. Wash the screen with cold water, using a power spray if possible. The mesh will appear stained and discolored, but it can be reused. Just make sure that all of the emulsion has been removed or it might interfere with the clarity of the next printed image.

Choosing and Using Color

Color plays a very important role in getting exciting results with any printing project. Therefore, it is wise to stop and take a look at the many dimensions of color. Knowing how to use color's language, moods, and symbolism to make a statement is especially important in the visual arts. Color is light and light is color. Color speaks. Color calms or excites. Color sells. Let's start with some basic definitions used to measure or express the dimensions of color.

Chroma: Greek for color, this term denotes the intensity of a hue.

Hue: Identifies a chroma or color by its name; for example, red, yellow, blue

Intensity / Saturation: A scale that measures the purity or brightness/dullness of a hue. Bright colors are higher on the scale of saturation (pure hue is the highest) while duller colors of the same hue are lower.

Value: The relative lightness (closer to white) or darkness (closer to black) of a hue; for example, yellow is light, so it is high in value, while violet is dark, or low in value.

Hues are divided into warm hues (from yellow to red-violet) and cool hues (from yellow-green to blue-violet). On a printing surface, warm colors appear to be closer to the viewer while cool colors appear to recede. Color always has a psychological effect on the viewer. This reaction depends on the viewer's sensitivity and life experience. For example, yellows and oranges evoke warmth and cheerfulness because of their association with the sun. Red, because of its connection to blood and fire, is perceived as violent, hot, and exciting. Blue, on the other hand, conjures up images of vastness and serenity, reminiscent of the sky and the sea. Green is restful. Violet is royal, ambiguous, and mysterious.

The basic way to describe colors and their relation to each other is by using the color wheel. Colors are divided into four categories: primary, secondary, intermediate, and tertiary colors. The primary colors are red, yellow, and blue. Primary colors cannot be made by mixing other colors. However, all other colors can be produced by mixing the three primaries along with white and black.

A secondary color is produced by mixing equal parts of two primaries. The three secondary colors include orange, which is obtained by mixing red and yellow; green, which appears when blue is mixed with yellow; and violet, which is born of red and blue.

(continued on page 21)

This sample shows transparent yellow ink printed on four different color papers. The yellow changes according to the color of the paper.

Intermediate colors are obtained by mixing adjoining primary and secondary colors, while tertiary colors come about when you mix two secondary colors. When white is added to a hue, it makes a tint of that hue; adding black produces a tone of the hue. A tone is a hue that has been muted. When muting a color, better results are achieved by mixing it with its complement. Muted colors convey calmness, tradition, and sophistication. Intense colors, on the other hand, convey youth, adventure, playfulness, and freedom. White, black, and gray are generally considered neutrals. Neutrals are pigments that show no color or chroma.

In general, screen prints can create a mood according to what color is printed next to another color. A print is usually done in several colorways or color combinations to serve a variety of tastes and moods. Color combinations are usually subject to purpose, culture, trends, and fashion, but there are some rules that lay the foundation for color harmony, meaning which colors work best together. For successful color combinations, start by choosing a color that works well with the color of the substrate while keeping in mind the client or purpose of the print. Then go to the color wheel and explore the many possibilities. For example, consider the amount of coverage each color will have within the design area.

There are six choices to consider and play with. These include monochromatic, complementary (direct or split), analogous and its variation, and triadic color combinations.

- A monochromatic combination happens when one hue is used throughout the print but is combined with different values (tints and/or tones) of the hue.

- A direct complementary color combination exists when two colors that are exactly opposite to each other on the color wheel are used. For example, yellow and violet make a direct complementary color combination.

- A split complementary combination uses not the complementary of a hue but the hues on either side of it. For example, yellow, blue, and red creates a split complementary color combination.

- Analogous harmonies of color occur when hues that are next to each other on the color wheel are printed together. The adjunct hues can be to the left, the right, or on either side of the first hue. For example: yellow, yellow-green, and yellow-orange or yellow, yellow-green, and green.

- A variation of the analogous combination occurs when the first hue is combined with its even-numbered neighbors. For example: yellow, green, and orange.

- Triadic color combinations are achieved by using hues that are equally spaced on the color wheel. For example: yellow, blue-green, and red-orange.

Finally, let it be said that there is the harmony of contrast in addition to the above harmonies of color. Contrast in color exists by comparing and bringing out the differences between two or more effects. Thus, in the field of color we have several kinds of contrast harmonies. There is the contrast of light and dark, as in black, white, and gray. There also is the contrast of cold and warm, as in red-orange and blue-green. Good color combinations can also be achieved by using the contrast of saturation—for example, the pure hue, a tint of it, and white, or the pure hue, a tone of the same, and black.

A multicolor design printed in repeat on a previously manipulated substrate

Basic Printing Methods

Screen printing has its origins in Japanese stenciling, but the process as we know it today probably began with the patents taken out by Samuel Simon in England at the turn of the twentieth century. He used silk stretched on frames to support hand-painted stencils; the same process was used by William Morris. In 1914, his idea was then adopted by John Pilsworth in San Francisco, California, who used a silk screen to form multi-color prints in much the same manner as silk screening is done today.

During World War I, screen printing took off as an industrial printing process in the United States; it was used first for flags and banners, and also for advertising in chain stores, which were beginning to appear. Around this time, the invention of the photographic stencil revolutionized the process. Subsequently, the quality of materials and inks used improved, but apart from the introduction of computer technology in the 1980s, very little else has changed since.

This section covers all the basic materials and methods, each presented through a simple creative project. Screen printing remains popular for several reasons: it is simple to learn and practice, versatile and forgiving, inexpensive and adaptable, fast and experimental, and rewarding and personal. With a screen, some paint, a squeegee, and the imagination, one can decorate any surface and transform any environment while having a blast doing it.

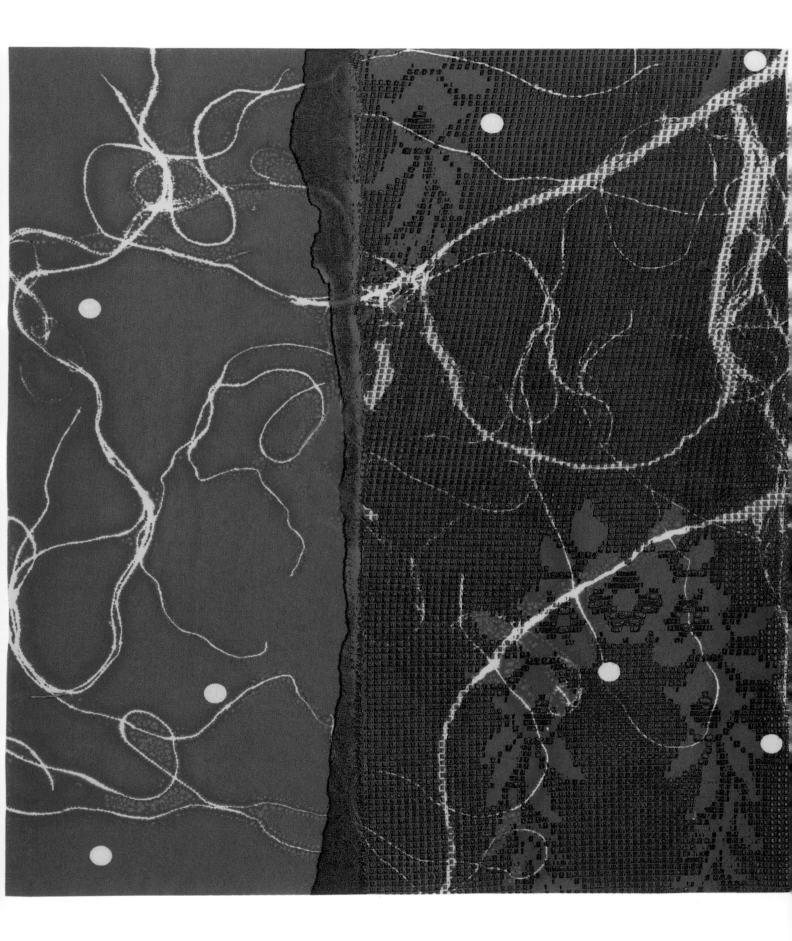

Simple Resist Printing

Y ou are now ready to start printing. As a first project we will do
something fun, easy, and colorful that yields bold and graphic
results. This is a resist print, which means that by using a variety of blocking materials during printing you will selectively stop the ink
from printing. The results can be used as a background for a later design
or stand alone nicely as simple artwork.

MATERIALS

- 110 count white-mesh screen
- squeegee (with the correct durometer and profile according to the substrate)
- water-based transparent inks in the three primary colors
- light-color substrate (cloth is recommended, but paper can be used as well)
- 2" (5 cm) -wide packaging tape
- resist materials: various sizes of masking tape to create stripes, stencils made out of paper or contact paper, strings, lace, leaves, and other flat objects to be placed between the mesh and the substrate (they will block out the ink during the printing process)
- clamps (optional)

Lace, strings, torn paper, and paper dots are used to create this
two-color resist print.

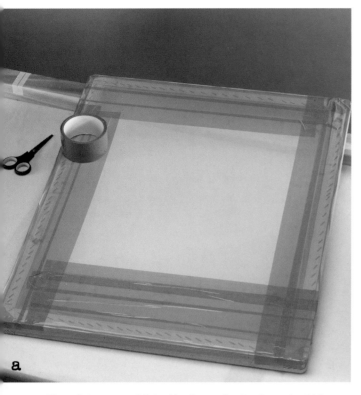

The print area established by the packaging tape should be smaller than the squeegee.

In taping the screen in preparation for inking, torn masking tape will create a soft edge along the print border if desired.

1. CREATING A PRINT AREA

Turn the screen upside down (printing side up, or the side that touches the substrate). Tape all four sides using the packaging tape. Make sure at least half of the frame is covered as well. This creates a printing area that should be smaller than the squeegee. Also, make sure to create a 3" to 4" (7.5 to 10 cm) negative (nonprinting) area all around the inside of the screen. This negative space, referred to as the inkwell, makes printing easy because it holds the ink and squeegee without touching the printing area (a).

2. TAPING THE SCREEN IN PREPARATION FOR INK

Flip the screen over (squeegee side up) and put one strip of tape all around the inside of the screen. This strip of tape prevents the ink from going between the mesh and the frame and makes cleaning the screen easier. It also prevents the inks from mixing with each other as you change colors using the

same screen. If you wish, instead of masking tape you can use duct tape, which will stay on the screen for a longer period of time (b).

3. STRETCHING THE SUBSTRATE ON THE PRINTING TABLE

For a paper substrate, spray a board with glue and press the paper on so that it stays flat during printing. Reinforce it by taping the edges as well.

For a fabric substrate, open the fabric and lay it on the printing table with the longest side of the cloth parallel to the length of the table. Use one or two T-pins to pin down one of the corners of the fabric. Then, take the opposite corner, pull it lightly, and pin it down. Now fill in with T-pins the whole length of the fabric in 2" to 3" (5 to 7.5 cm) intervals. Make sure that the pins face the center of the table and that they go all the way in and don't stick out. After this is done, take the third corner, pull it lightly and pin it down. Fill in this

c

Carefully stretch the substrate on the printing table so no wrinkles affect or interfere with the printing process.

d

Arrange the desired resist materials where the color of the substrate is to remain.

side with pins the same way, without pulling or stretching the fabric. Finally, take the fourth corner, pull it lightly, and pin it down.

Pin the two other sides of the fabric the same way, but with one variation. This time pull and stretch the material before pinning it down. The objective is to get rid of any wrinkles the fabric might have, so it stays flat and taut under the screen while printing (c).

4. MIXING THE INKS

If you are mixing your own inks, you'll need several plastic containers with lids. Start by putting approximately 32 ounces (950 ml) of the base in a container. The exact amount depends on the number of prints and the area of coverage. Then go to the pigment containers and using drops of each pigment, mix the colors needed—in this case the three primaries (red, blue, and yellow). It is easier to build the intensity of the color by starting low on the scale of saturation.

Otherwise you risk wasting your materials. Keep in mind that the color will appear a shade lighter after it dries than it appears while wet.

Also, remember that yellow is the weakest pigment among transparent, water-based inks. Adding a bit of extra pigment or a touch of red or even a drop of white might give it some depth. Too much white, however, will make it opaque.

5. PREPARING THE RESIST

Resist material can be adhered either to the substrate or directly onto the mesh. If the mesh is used, make sure it is adhered to the printing side of the screen. Adhering anything on the squeegee side will interfere with printing and will eventually be removed by the motion of the squeegee. Place the first resist material where the color of the substrate is to be kept as is. Also cover the areas where the other two primaries are to be printed in their pure color (d).

Choosing which color to print first can hinge on the effect desired.

Printing the second color

6. INKING THE FIRST COLOR

Place the screen on the substrate and print the first of the primaries; let's say the red. If you plan to overlap (or "trap") colors, print the darkest color first and then get progressively lighter, avoiding any black or opaque pigments (e).

7. PRINTING THE SECOND COLOR

After the first color is printed, put the excess ink back in the container and wash the screen with cold water. Do so gently if you want to keep any resist material adhered to the mesh.

Printing the next of the colors can be done while the first print is still wet; this is known as printing wet on wet. The colors mix with each other better by printing wet on wet, which might be good in some cases. However, keep in mind that some of the first color will become weak since it will adhere to the mesh and be lifted off the print. Also, the screen might move while being placed on the wet print, resulting in a smudged print. If you are new to screen printing, you may wish to let the previous colors dry before printing the next one.

Once the screen and frame are completely dry (from washing), place the frame on the print after the red areas have been covered, and the blue areas have been uncovered. Repeat the printing steps this time with blue pigment, then save the ink in its container and clean the screen. By now you have printed a composition of large shapes, consisting of red, blue, and areas of purple where blue was printed over red (f).

8. PRINTING THE THIRD COLOR

Continue printing with yellow after everything has dried and the areas with pure substrate, blue, red, and purple have been covered. By the end of printing, your composition should reveal the color of the original substrate (which becomes more obvious after trimming the print), the three primaries, three secondaries, and even triadic colors and/or different values of the primaries and secondaries. The results depend on the shape and manipulation of the resist material and the quality of the primary colors. It's always a good idea to print more than one print and create several copies or variations of the same composition (g).

g

Add paper and mesh resists to each half of the design.

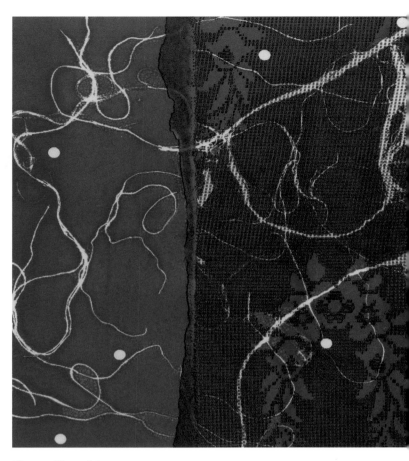

The resulting print

Basic Printing Guidelines

If this is the first time you're printing, follow these directions carefully:

Place squeegee in the inkwell of the screen at the top or the bottom. **The squeegee stays in the screen the entire time of printing.**

Place a generous amount of ink in front of the squeegee the entire length of the printing area. **When printing starts, there must a sufficient amount of ink in front of the squeegee as it is pulled over the printing area or some areas will print and others will not.**

It is very important the screen does not move while printing or the print will be bleary. **Use a clamp to secure the screen on the printing table or place a bar (a piece of 2 x 4 wood will do) at the edge of the printing table. Place and hold the screen against the bar while**

pulling the squeegee toward you. If screen is secured with a clamp, both hands can pull the squeegee while printing. In some cases, since it does not need a tremendous amount of pressure for the ink to pass through, you can hold and press down the screen with one hand and print with the other.

Hold the squeegee at a 45-degree angle and pull it while pressing the ink through the mesh over the entire printing area and then back. **The amount of passes (pulls) varies according to the size of the mesh, the angle of the squeegee, the pressure applied, the viscosity of the ink, and—of course—the quality of the substrate. For example, if printing on paper one pass might be enough. Thin fabric might need two passes, and heavy fabric, four. The more passes, the thicker the deposited ink, and sometimes the darker its color.**

VARIATION IDEAS

Experimenting with simple resist materials and basic color choices can yield bold and elegant results.

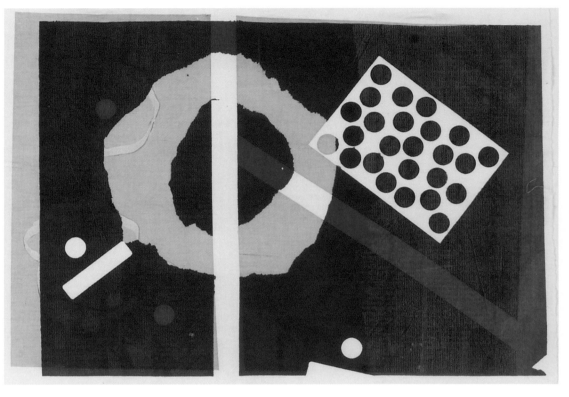

A simple resist print on fabric using tapes, torn paper, and perforated paper

A variation of the print above

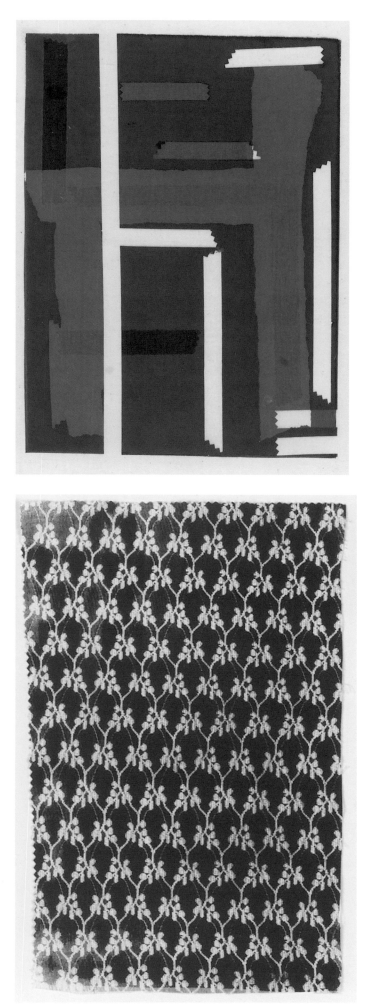

A chair print on paper with masking tape used as the resist material

A mask print is easily created also using masking tape as a resist.

A simple resist print on cloth. A piece of lace is stretched on white fabric and red ink is printed over through the mesh of a screen.

Four-step print series on fabric

Direct Block-Out Screen Printing

In the first project, we experimented with very quick non-permanent stencils. This time, we'll employ a more permanent stencil—one that can be printed over and over again to produce multiple images in many different colors. This printing technique, which is known as reduction printing, is ideal for creating stunning place mats, decorative pillows, tote bags, and T-shirts, among other things.

MATERIALS

- a water-resistant medium such as screen filler liquid or a sensitized photo emulsion

- a couple of bristle brushes (flats, brights, or rounds) in sizes according to the lines of the design and the area to be covered

- two hinge clamps, tailor's chalk, or two pieces of 2 x 4 nailed together to create an L-shaped corner

Using a direct block-out process, this T-shirt and tote bag were screen printed in a one-color design.

a

b

Applying first resist for this three-color reduction print. The beauty of this method is the rich texture and brushstroke effect of the print.

Printing yellow as the first color of this design

The hinge clamps, tailor's chalk, or pieces of wood used in this project create a simple registration system needed for the reduction technique. By marking the exact position of the screen, it is possible to go back onto what has already been printed and manipulate the design by adding colors or selectively printing certain areas. Bold lines and rich textures are ideal for this technique. This is not a stencil for fine-detailed designs; leave those designs for the photo technique.

1. PREPARING THE DESIGN

To draw a design for this project, place the screen on the drawing, squeegee side up, and copy the design with a soft pencil onto the mesh. (A hard pencil's point may go through the mesh and make a hole.) By drawing directly onto the mesh with a water-resistant medium you will produce a direct stencil that yields prints rich in textures with beautiful brushstrokes.

2. APPLYING THE FIRST LAYER OF FILLER

Now turn the screen printing side up and use your paintbrush and filler or emulsion to start filling in the negative areas. You don't want to cover much of the mesh with the filler before printing your first color. Remember that these areas will remain the color of the substrate throughout the printing process. You will notice that the design is, and should be, in reverse. If there are words in the design they should be upside down so they read correctly when screen is in the printing position.

Do not apply the filler too thickly. If the liquid used is water-based screen filler, you are ready to print the first color of the design as soon as the filler dries. However, if sensitized photo emulsion has been used, it has to be fixed by exposing it to a strong light source. This will ensure that it becomes permanent and withstands the washing of the screen when the color changes (a).

Reducing the printing area by drawing with emulsion

Printing the second color

3. SECURING AND REGISTERING YOUR MATERIALS

Before the first color is printed, make sure the substrate is pinned down on the printing table and its position is marked. The position of the screen on the substrate should be marked as well. You can use tape to mark the corners of the screen, tailor's chalk to draw lines on the substrate, or the L-shaped corner as a guide. If clamps are used, fasten two of them on the printing table (or on a piece of plywood separated from the printing table) at a distance smaller than one of the sides on the frame. Then mark the place on the frame where the screen is held by the clamps.

This is an excellent way of changing screens quickly without losing registration. The objective is to be able to go back in the same spot and continue printing (in registration) with a new color and a changed stencil.

4. PRINTING THE FIRST COLOR

Print the first color. Make as many copies of the one-color design as you like (b). Remove the screen, wash the color off with cold water, and let it dry. After the screen is dry, turn the printing side up and reduce the printing area by applying with your brush more blocked-out liquid lines, shapes, and other elements relating to the main design. What is being drawn now will remain the color of the first print, and everything around it will change to a new color produced by the mixing of the two printed colors.

After the new layer of filler or block-out is dried and fixed, follow the steps previously described and add the second color. This can be repeated until there is no more negative space to be filled (d).

5. RECLAIMING THE SCREEN

When all the printing is done, you can reclaim the mesh by removing the filler. Screen filler is removed by wetting both sides of the screen with a liquid detergent soap and letting it stand in a horizontal position for ten minutes. Then spray it with warm water. A stiff scrub brush might make the job easier. Photo emulsion is removed by using a commercial reclaiming liquid or bleach. This stencil can be used over and over again unless the reduction technique is used and the stencil gets filled up progressively and eventually is destroyed. However, the screen can still be reclaimed and rinsed (e).

For drama, depth, and three-dimensional looks, opaque colors as well as metallic and black can be used as the negative space decreases.

Final layer of emulsion is applied

Using Screen Drawing Fluid

To create a variation on the direct block-out technique, use a water-based screen drawing fluid. In this case, the lines of the design to be printed are drawn with a brush on the printing side of the screen with the drawing fluid. What is drawn will eventually print. After the drawing fluid is completely dry, evenly cover the entire mesh of the screen with a thin coat of the screen filler using a brush or a piece of cardboard. When the screen filler is completely dry, spray the screen on both sides with cold water until the drawing fluid is dissolved. This opens the areas of the design and allows the ink to go through during printing.

The beauty of the reduction printing technique is that it yields designs with exciting and bold brush strokes as well as rich textural effects and multiple colors, while requiring only one screen.

A two-color design printed in a repeat that creates a variety of stripes. By selectively trapping, or layering, the two colors, a third color emerges that adds yet another element of interest to this geometric design.

Basic Elements of Design

Design, whether it be structural or decorative, is the process of putting various elements into an order to produce a coherent unit. Structural design deals with the way things are made, while decorative design deals with the way they are beautified or enhanced. In screen printing we are dealing strictly with decorative design, specifically with surface design. By organizing lines, shapes, color, and pattern to create a unit of images, we can decorate a surface and make a visual statement.

Line: To some, a line is a series of spots connected to each other; to others, a line is a point in motion. Either way you look at it, a line is the most basic element of design. It has qualities that are very personal and depend on the materials used and the expertise of the user. It can also suggest movement, rhythm, calmness, action, distance, activity, and stability, to mention just a few.

Lines become symbols, give direction and emphasis to a design, create patterns and textures, and almost always create an emotional reaction in the viewer. Horizontal lines, for example, evoke majesty and strength, while vertical lines imply calmness and balance. Curved lines suggest femininity, and diagonal lines demand attention and involvement, thus seeming aggressive, dynamic, and energetic. Optical illusions can be achieved by combining lines of different directions and qualities.

Form or Shape: As a moving point travels, it marks an area with a particular shape or form. In other words, shape is the outline of a form. The space this shape occupies is its mass. Shape is two-dimensional, therefore, and mass is three-dimensional. In surface design, mass is volume and is indicated by shading. Shapes are usually divided into these categories: natural, geometric, nonobjective, and abstract.

Natural shapes are those of humans, animals, plants, and their parts and products. Geometric shapes are those that define space accurately and with mathematical precision. Nonobjective shapes are shapes that do not represent anything from the natural world. Abstract shapes are shapes that have been taken from nature and purposely distorted. This distortion can be partial, in which case the object is still recognizable, or total, when the object becomes a nonobjective shape.

Pattern: When an element or a unit of elements in a design is repeated at regular intervals, it creates a pattern. A pattern on a surface creates a sense of movement and rhythm while establishing balance and unity in a composition.

A designer uses all or some of the above elements to create a two-dimensional structure or unit that is referred to as a composition. A good composition should have a variety of elements yet still maintain order and unity. Without variety and unity a composition is lacking and confusing. Interesting compositions typically contain dominant elements that are emphasized, subordinate elements that work with and complement the dominant elements, and accents for pleasant surprises.

Designers never take the placement of an object as an arbitrary action. The negative space is always considered in making a powerful visual statement.

This one-color linear design is printed with a warm, earthy brown ink that complements the color and texture of the natural linen fabric it is printed on.

One-Color Simple Repeat Design

C hoosing to create a one-color design can resolve issues related to project cost, storage space, and production time. When creating a one-color design, keep in mind the following: the composition of shapes and forms; a variety of patterns and textures; the play of light and dark, as well as positive and negative space; and the variation of lines that suggest movement and create depth.

MATERIALS

- a 15" x 18" (38 x 46 cm) clear prepared or frosted (matte) acetate. Vellum can also be used.
- opaque markers or black India ink and a sable brush
- a 20" x 20" (51 x 51 cm) (or larger) sheet of graph paper
- a soft pencil
- a 20" (51 cm) ruler
- frosted adhesive tape
- masking tape
- tracing paper

Positive artwork on paper

a

Painting a positive with opaque ink on tracing paper

b

Drawing registration marks on tracing paper aids ensures properly aligned repeats.

1. PREPARING A POSITIVE

In screen printing, a positive is the artwork that is ready to be transferred or photographed to a screen. A positive is made by using a clear or translucent base, upon which opaque markings or designs have been drawn or otherwise affixed. Opaque areas, whether they are fine dots, lines, or bold shapes, will print. Clear areas will not print. A positive, by being photographed on the sensitized mesh, produces a negative (the screen), which in turn produces— through printing—an unlimited number of positives or prints.

There are many different ways of making a positive. The choice depends on the individual, the available materials, and the desired results. Positives can be done entirely by hand, by photocopying, or by using the computer. They also can be done by mixing two or even all of these methods.

To hold the opaque medium, a base of acetate, vellum, or others such as Mylar, tracing paper, copy paper, or even glass should be used. The opaque medium itself can be anything from black India ink to gouache, opaque markers, lithographers crayons, China markers, tapes, stickers, construction paper, or any variety of other materials, as long as the medium is opaque in either its color or composition. Different drawing techniques can be used to achieve interesting looks. Besides brushes, stamps also can be used. Mix thin and thick lines and solid brushstrokes as well as dry-brush effects (a).

The size of the positive design always depends on the size of the screen being used. For this example, a 10" x 14" (25.4 x 35.6 cm) size design is used. Take a piece of tracing paper and then by using the graph paper mark the corner of a 10" x 14" (25.4 x 35.6 cm) area with a soft pencil.

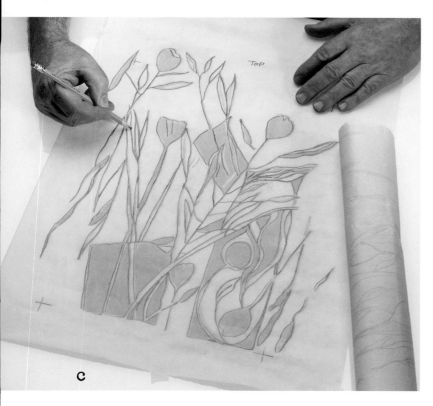

c

d

Make all corrections on one of the copies and keep it as your master drawing. If the tracing paper is to become the positive, make the design opaque by going over the image with an opaque marker or brush and opaque ink.

Place a one-color design into a simple repeat by tiling tracings and fixing the spacing between them.

Mark only the corners where the lines meet, not the whole line. These small crosses are referred to as the *registration marks* (b).

Next fill the area with the design and identify one of the sides as the top of the design by writing the word "top" on the paper (c). This is a directional top, not a visual one. Take another piece of tracing paper and make a tracing of the design including the registration marks and the word "top." By using the registration marks and the top, place the copies next to each other and check the area where they meet (d).

Add more design if there is an empty space where the design repeats, or erase areas that over-lap. The design is now in a simple repeating pattern that can be tiled to create a border or frieze.

Tracing Paper vs. Acetate

Tracing paper as a positive has some limitations. One of them is that it can be torn easily as it is being handled. Another is that it does not lie down very flat, especially after large areas of ink have been drawn on it. Acetate makes a better and longer lasting positive. When using acetate, the design can be photocopied or drawn directly on it. Small pieces of photocopied acetate or vellum can be taped together to make up the desired size of positive. If you choose to draw, place the acetate on the design and tape it down so it does not move. With a soft pencil, copy the registration marks and the word *top*. The pencil will not show on prepared acetate.

Taping the artwork to the screen is another way of matching artwork and screen. Art is taped with clear tape and is in reverse.

Measuring the distance between prints

2. REGISTERING A POSITIVE TO THE SCREEN

Registering the positive to the screen gives total control to the printer especially if the printing is to be done in repeat. As mentioned before, there are many ways to register screens to positives. Let's look at yet another one.

A.   Draw a straight line the length of the printing table, placing masking or duct tape along the whole length. For a more permanent setup, a straight piece of 2 x 4 lumber can be nailed, glued, or simply held in place with C-clamps on the printing table, thus creating a sturdy bar the screen can be placed against.

B.   Measure one of the sides of the frame and draw a line at the center of it right onto the wood.

C.   Take the positive and pin it or tape it on the printing table at a parallel line to the tape or wood and at a distance of 6" to 8" (15 to 20 cm) from it. Use the registration marks to measure the distance (e).

D.   Find the center of the design and draw a vertical line at that point on the tape or wood.

E.   Take the screen and place it on the positive, matching the line drawn on its frame with the line on the tape or wood on the printing table.

F.   With a ruler and a soft pencil, copy the registration marks and the word "top" onto the mesh.

G.   Finally, coat the screen with emulsion and let it dry.

3. PHOTOGRAPHING A SCREEN WITH THE REGISTERED POSITIVE

Once the screen has dried, take the positive and tape it on the glass of the exposure unit right side up. Then place the dried screen on top of the positive, making sure that the registration marks of the screen match those of the positive and that the "top" of both is the same. Keeping the screen in place, weight it down under a felt-covered board and then expose it to light as described on page 60.

4. PRINTING IN REPEAT

A.   At about 5" (12.7 cm) from the bar on the printing table and parallel to it, stretch the substrate as described on page 26.

B.   Place the screen on the substrate where the first print is to be printed, and draw a line on the bar that corresponds to the line on the frame of the screen.

C.   Turn the screen printing side up and measure the repeat or the distance between prints (f).

Preparing to print a one-color simple repeat by measuring and marking the repeat, the intervals at which the image is going to be printed

Secure the screen against the printing bar before pulling the print. By matching the lines drawn both on the frame of the screen and the printing bar, an accurate and fluent repeat is achieved.

D. Draw lines on the bar at the repeat distance starting from the first line, which is the beginning. For example, if the repeat is 15" (38.1 cm), draw lines on the bar every 15" (38.1 cm) the whole length of the desired printing (g). This is because the size of the design in the screen is repeated, not the size of the screen.

E. Place the ink in the inkwell, on the top of the screen, and print pulling towards you. Because the screen is secured against the bar and it's not going to move, you can use two hands to pull (h).

F. As the printing is done, skip one line and print every other one, allowing the ink to dry between prints.

G. Clean the screen and let it dry. Then, go back and fill in the missing prints.

H. If there is no time to do steps f and g, be very careful when printing the ink between wet spots. Make sure the screen is in place before putting it down, and once it is down, do not move it, just print it. The areas of the screen that touch the wet print will pick up some of the ink and make them lighter. In that case, make sure the ink that was lifted off the wet area is wiped off or it will leave a "ghost" print.

A one-color repeat design that shows a border

Two variations of a one-color design printed in repeat on two previously manipulated substrates. Rubbings from different coins inspired the design.

This one-color design, inspired by the inside of a church, was printed in the off-registration technique on white fabric with blotches of color printed over it.

This print on fabric combines the simple resist technique (for the background) and a one-color photo screen image (for the faces).

This simple resist print on woven fabric was created using the rainbow squeegee printing technique. It can easily be used as a place mat or a decorative pillowcase.

Rainbow Squeegee Printing Technique

Instead of printing with one color in the screen, several colors can be printed simultaneously. This printing technique is known as the rainbow squeegee because all seven colors of the rainbow can be created by placing the three primaries (red, yellow, blue) next to each other in a screen and then printing.

Before the first pull, mix the colors gently where they run into each other to get a good secondary color. No two pulls are ever alike with this technique because the colors mix and change as you print. If a long piece of cloth is to be printed, the colors might get too muddy at some point. In that case, stop printing, clean and dry the screen, and then reapply clean colors.

Printing a Multicolor Design

This pomegranate pattern is a multicolor blotch print made into a place mat and napkin set. The base fabric is white cotton.

In order to create a multicolor design, you must learn color separation. In screen printing, a screen and a positive are needed for each color of the design. So, if a design has five colors, five positives are made, and eventually five screens, each carrying one of the colors of the design. This step of the process is called color separation, and it can be done by hand or by computer. For the colors to print correctly during printing, the positives and eventually the screens must be calibrated to each other in advance. This step is called registration, and it's done by using registration marks. These markings help align the various positives that make up the design so they print easily and correctly while producing a multicolored print.

MATERIALS

- two (or more) screens stretched with the appropriate mesh
- tracing paper (optional) and a sheet of graph paper that is slightly larger than the design to be used
- transparent color markers
- opaque medium such as markers, inks, or paints
- prepared or frosted acetate, vellum, or tracing paper
- register marks
- soft pencil and a ruler
- sensitized photo emulsion

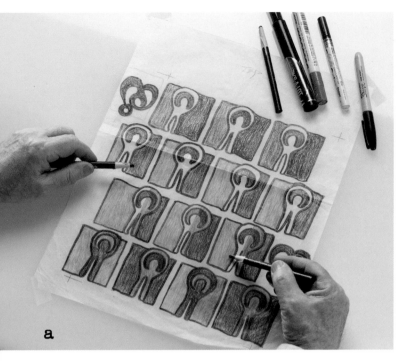

a

This drawing shows the placement of two colors of the design and where they overlap to create a third color.

b

Color separation begins by painting one of the colors on the first acetate.

c

Painting the second positive of a two-color design

REGISTRATION DONE BY HAND

For this project we will use two colors (two screens) and the trapping (or overlapping) of these two colors to create a third color.

1. Draw the design on tracing paper with a pencil. If preferred, it can also be a photocopied collage of various images. This will be the master or working drawing of the image to be printed, and the size of the image will depend on the size of the screens being used.

2. After the image is drawn, indicate where the colors go by using the colored markers (a).

3. As the colors are applied on the drawing, the areas where the two colors overlap receive two applications of color.

4. When this is done, place the drawing over the graph paper and draw registration marks at the corners of where the straight lines that contain the design meet. Mark the top of the design as well.

5. Place a piece of acetate on the design and tape it down so it does not move. Peel off the precut registration marks and place them on the acetate on

Print of a two color design in repeat. The visual spacing between repeats can be adjusted by reducing the repeat distance.

top of the registration marks drawn on the graph paper. Also mark the top of the design on the acetate. Then, place a second piece of acetate down and do the same.

6. Color separation can now begin. With an opaque marker, paint, or ink, draw all the areas of the first color of the design, including the trapped areas (b).

7. Remove the first acetate and on the second one paint the other color of the design including the trapped areas (c).

8. Each color of this two-color design is on a different positive, and the two positives register to each other with the help of the register marks. The color separation by hand is now done.

Halftones and Digitally Made Positives

As mentioned before, positives can be created in many different ways. The fastest and easiest way to do that today is by using a computer and an image manipulation program such as Adobe Photoshop.

This software allows you to import an image into the computer, alter it in size, color, composition, and other visual aspects as well as technical possibilities, and then print the results on vellum, acetate, or paper. This printout can be used a positive for printing.

Regardless of how the positive is made, the concept remains the same: opaque areas will print, clear areas will not. Another important technical detail—all artwork used for screen printing is characterized as either line art or halftone art. Line art is in the form of solid areas or lines, while halftone art is composed of dotted lines. The size of the dots and the distance between them determine the amount of solid color they represent. Also, the number of dots in a straight line of an inch determines the line count.

That is to say that if there are 50 dots in a one-inch line, it is a "50 line" tone or 50 lpi. A positive with 50 lines to a square inch would have 2,500 dots (50 lpi x 50 lpi) per square inch, or dpi. This number is the average that can be handled with screen printing.

When printing halftones, the angles should be considered to avoid what is called a moiré effect. This is a special distortion of the image that occurs when the angle of the dots corresponds with the angle of the openings in the mesh, creating a pattern in the printed ink, rather than a solid color. To avoid this, select an angle that is a minimum of 4 degrees offset to a maximum of 8 degrees offset. You can do this in Adobe Photoshop or any other image manipulation program.

Samples of digitally produced positives

Registering screens for a multicolor design

REGISTRATION OF SCREENS
TO POSITIVES

Once the color separation is done and the positives have been produced, the screens have to be marked to (or registered to) the acetate. All screens are marked from the same acetate regardless of their number, so choose the one that shows most of the design and use it to mark all of the screens. Go to the bar you have built on the printing table and by using the straight line between two registration marks, pin or tape the positive on the table at about 4" to 5" (10–12 cm) from the bar. The positive must be right side up (facing you).

Mark the first screen as described on page 44. Without moving anything, take the second screen, place it in exactly the same place as the one before and mark it as well (d).

In the same way, mark the third and fourth screens if, let's say, the design is a four-color design. Then, coat the screens with emulsion. When the emulsion is dry, photograph or burn the image following the steps outlined on page 60.

This sample shows the two colors printed separately and together to form a design

PRINTING IN REGISTRATION

When printing a design that has more than one color, registration becomes paramount. To achieve good registration:

1. Pin the substrate very tautly so it does not move under the screen during printing. It should stay in exactly the same place until all colors have been printed.

2. No matter what type of registration method is used, markings should be clearly visible, accurately measured, and marked so the screens go in exactly the same place for each color of the design.

3. If colors are to be layered to get a third color, print the darker of the colors first and then the lighter. If that is not the objective, then print from lighter to darker.

4. In repeating a multicolor color design, prepare the substrate and set the stops or measurements of the repeat as described on pages 44–45.

5. Print the first color throughout the number of repeats and let it dry. Without moving a thing, go in the exact same spots as before and print the second or third or fourth screens or colors.

Creating a Blotch Print

A blotch print is a direct way of printing an image on a substrate by printing the background of the image to define the design by the areas that do not print. The nonprinted areas remain the original color of the substrate in the desired image or pattern. Other colors then can be added within these areas to produce a multicolor blotch design.

In putting a blotch into repeat, the background is treated as a design, and the joining of the repeat occurs in the negative areas of the design, not the background. With hand screen printing, a repeat is never done in an area of color but always in areas where there is no printing. One of the limitations of hand-screen-printing is that color areas cannot be repeated or joined with success. For example, it is impossible to hand-screen-print long, solid-color stripe designs. So in solving the problem, the designer must include other design elements such as lines or shapes that would allow the break for the repeat.

A blotch print might be used to imitate a chemically produced discharge print (see pages 80–81). Blotch prints on fabric, with large areas of pigment print, usually produce a fabric with a stiff touch or "hand."

Shells and other shapes from the world of the sea inspired this blotch design, printed in repeat. By manipulating the substrate as well as the screen during printing, the print looks like a multicolor design.

Making a Photographic Screen with Found Objects

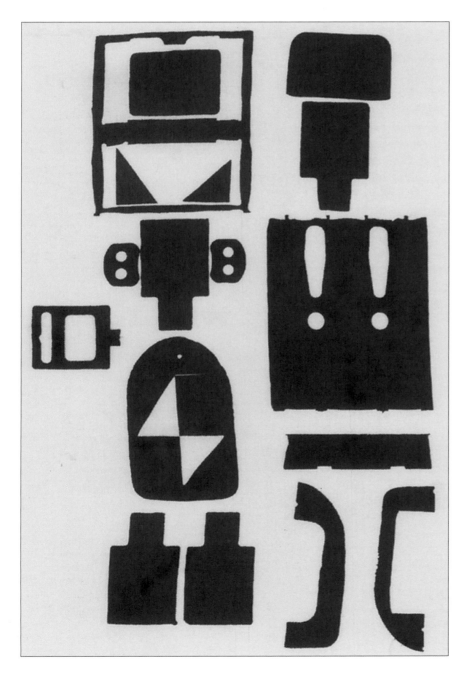

This print, "Standing Couple," was made using found objects as a positive. Anything that is flat and opaque can be used. By using your imagination, compositions ranging from humorous to surreal can be achieved.

Using everyday objects such as string, gears, buttons, and almost anything else you can fit on a screen, you can produce an incredible array of interesting and unique prints. Because found objects are usually opaque and have no details, this is a very easy photo screen to produce. After gathering your materials, the first step is to prepare the screen with photo emulsion.

MATERIALS

- a screen with 110 or 10xx mesh
- a scoop coater to apply emulsion on the screen
- sensitized diazo photo emulsion
- exposure unit or other light source
- a timer that counts seconds and minutes
- clear tape
- a sheet of clear or frosted acetate
- thin ($\frac{1}{16}$" [2 mm]), flat, and opaque objects to create a found object design

Stencils created photographically with found objects result in silhouette-like images that are similar to photograms, the shadowlike images first produced by artists such as Man Ray and Moholy Nagy in the 1920s.

Coating a screen with photo emulsion

APPLYING EMULSION TO THE SCREEN

1. If the screen is being used for the first time, wash it with a degreaser to rinse off any finishes that might interfere with the adhesion of the emulsion. You can also use soap and warm water if a degreaser is not available. Let the screen dry in a dust-free room.

2. Place the screen tilted against a wall, printing side facing out. Take a cup of sensitized emulsion and place it in the scoop coater along the whole length of it. Use the sharper side of the scoop and place it against the mesh at the bottom of the screen. Tilt the scoop and wait until the emulsion is touching the mesh at the whole length of the screen. Then by using both hands and pressing, take the scoop to the top of the screen (a).

3. This motion will leave a thin layer of emulsion behind as the scoop travels to the top. The angle at which the scoop is held is very important. Too much of an angle will leave behind a thick layer, which is not desired in most cases. Stop when you reach the end of the screen, but do not lessen the pressure. Move the scoop slowly from left to right while pressing and trying to put the excess emulsion back into the scoop. The objective is to get an even, thin layer of emulsion to cover the mesh.

4. Use small pieces of cardboard to clean the edges of the emulsion but never touch the area where the image is going to be photographed with anything. Hold the screen up to a light source and see if the emulsion has covered the mesh well.

5. Sometimes a second coat is needed because the first one was not applied correctly and there are a lot of pinholes that the light shines through. The second coat can be applied immediately (wet on wet) over the first one. It can also be applied after the first one has dried. A second layer of emulsion (you can apply as many as four layers) makes a stronger stencil that will increase the sharpness of the image as well. The second layer can be applied from the squeegee side of the screen, thus enclosing the mesh between two layers of emulsion. Let the screen dry in a horizontal position, printing side up, in a dust-free room and wait at least half an hour before photographing it.

CREATING A FOUND OBJECT COMPOSITION

1. While the emulsion is drying in a dark place, make a composition with the found objects on a piece of acetate. Secure them with clear tape.

2. Bring the composition to the exposure unit and tape it in the middle of the glass (b).

Tips for Working with Emulsion

■ Avoid thickly applied emulsion, which may peel off while developing the screen.

■ Layers of emulsion require longer exposures.

■ Screens may be coated with diazo emulsions in advance and used as needed if they are kept in a dark, dry, and cool place.

■ Emulsion becomes light sensitive after drying.

■ Always read and consult with the manufacturer's information and the MSDS on the emulsion being used.

■ Sensitized emulsion can be stored up to seven weeks at room temperature and up to four months if kept in a refrigerator.

b

Found objects arranged on acetate and positioned over an exposure unit

Center the screen over the composition.

Weight the screen with plywood covered in felt.

3. Place the screen on top of the acetate and center the composition in the middle of the screen (c).

4. To weight the screen against the surface of the objects, place in the screen a piece of plywood that is smaller than the inside of the screen and is covered with some felt. It is important that there is direct contact between the sensitized mesh and the found objects or the light will escape and the definition of the shapes will be fuzzy. Place weights on the plywood to increase the contact if needed (d).

5. Turn the light on to expose the screen. The exposure time depends on the emulsion being used and the number of layers applied to the mesh (see A Test for Determining Exposure Time, page 61).

6. Develop the screen after exposure by wetting both sides with a gentle spray of cold water. This stops the reaction of the emulsion to light. Wait about a minute and then continue washing the screen until all unexposed emulsion (which looks like white foam) has dissolved and washed away, thus creating a stencil (e).

7. Let the screen dry thoroughly, then prepare it for printing as described on page 26. After the screen is taped, check it for pinholes. Pinholes are tiny openings on the screen caused by dust on the mesh or the glass on the exposure unit, the emulsion itself, or the air where the screen was placed to dry. Pinholes can also result when the emulsion is not applied properly, the screen is underexposed during exposure time, or the screen is overwashed during developing.

   Pinholes are hard to detect until the screen is checked by holding it against a light source or by making a test print on a piece of plain white paper. Pinholes will ruin the design unless they are covered either with tape if they are away from the design area or by filling them with emulsion (f).

Develop the screen after exposure.

f

Touching up the pinholes is done on the printing side of the screen by using a round bristle #6 (or smaller) brush for areas near the design or a piece of cardboard for other areas. The brush must be washed immediately after being used. The touched-up areas have to be fixed (after they air dry) by exposing the screen to light before printing starts.

A Test for Determining Exposure Time

During exposure, light travels, and where there is nothing to stop it from reaching the emulsion, those areas become water insoluble and permanent. The areas where the found object stopped the light from reaching the emulsion remain water soluble and wash away.

Many factors can affect exposure time: multiple layers, the kind of mesh, the distance from the light source, the opaqueness of the objects, and, of course, the quality of the light source. Are you using a point light source such as metal halide or carbon arch lamp, or is your light fluorescent? (With point light source, rays come from one single bulb, which is much better than clusters of fluorescent bulbs.)

To make sure you get the correct exposure, use this quick and easy test. Expose a test screen for one minute then cover half of it with black construction paper and expose it again for another minute. This cover/uncover method can be done repeatedly, up to five different exposure times. Mark each strip with the corresponding amount of exposure time. Wash the exposed screen and pick the section that gave the best resolution to determine the correct exposure time.

VARIATION IDEAS

VARIATION #1:
PRINTING OFF-REGISTRATION

For this technique, the printing is controlled by registering the screen as described on pages 44 and 53. A light color is printed first. The screen is then washed and dried. When the first color has dried as well, the screen is placed on top of the print and purposely moved as much as half an inch (or less) to the right or left before the second color is printed.

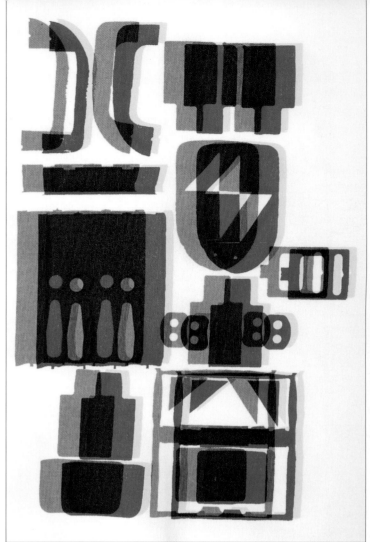

Variations of the off-registration printing technique

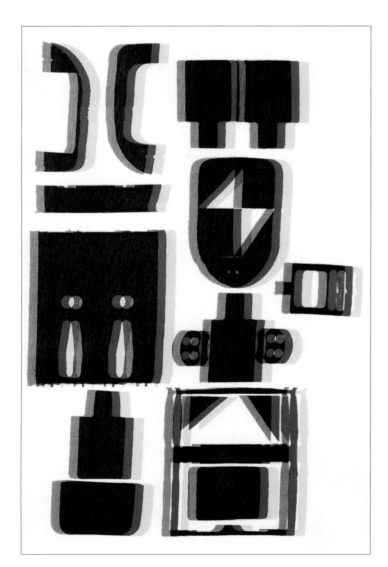

A found object screen, printed slightly off registration. Using a color darker than the initial tone adds dimension to the design by creating a shadow effect.

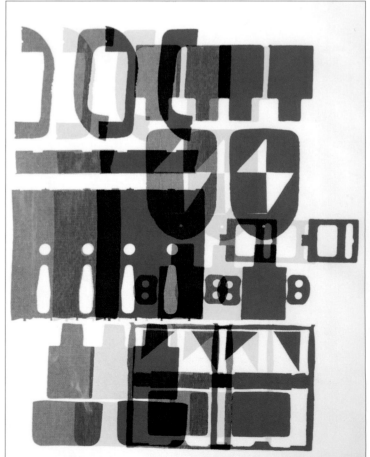

VARIATION #2:
ADDING THE REDUCTION TECHNIQUE

The off-registration technique allows experimentation with color-layering effects. After all printing is done and before the screen is reclaimed, you can also try the reduction technique with your stencil.

Reducing the printing area of a photo screen with emulsion

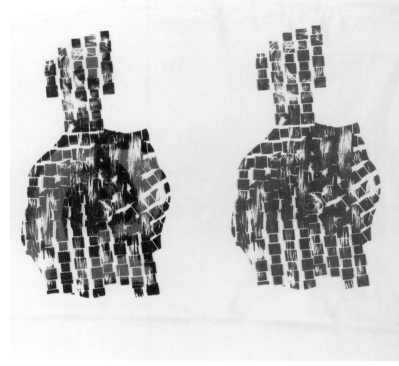

"Torso" variation of the reduction printing technique with a photographically made screen

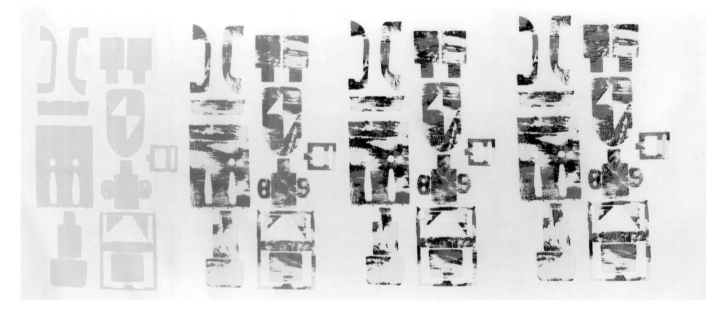

A three-step reduction print of the found-objects photo screen

Special Topics

This section covers a variety of specialized techniques and effects that can be achieved with screen printing. We will explore printing on T-shirts, how to exploit the power of black-and-white design, how to print on dark substrates, how to use specialized inks, how to print by removing color (discharge printing), how to print textures, and how to print on paper. A wide selection of sample work will illustrate all these types of printing, along with unique variations and clever combinations of print techniques.

Printing can communicate our essence and our involvement in the community of mankind. We choose the colors, patterns, and surfaces on which they are presented. We can create our own garment styles, customize our environments, and express our opinions. Screen printing can be used to create beautiful and personal gifts, and offers the gift of being creative.

A photographic screen of a texture printed on gray fabric several times, each time changing the color and direction of the image. The technique produces a rich-looking surface with interesting patinas.

Printing on T-Shirts

"New York, New York!," a commemorative T-shirt; this Manhattan cityscape is very familiar. But, the addition of the texture printed in blue and red, and used as a frame, is what makes this T-shirt unique and personal.

In the field of garment decoration there is nothing more popular and enduring than the printed T-shirt. No business, association, organization, or club passes on the opportunity of using the T-shirt to promote itself or to let its message be known. So it's no wonder that people acquire large T-shirt collections and still want more.

MATERIALS

- light-colored T-shirt
- thin plywood or non-corrugated board
- spray adhesive or T-pins
- screen with 110 (10xx) or less mesh count
- water-based textile inks
- a medium (60–70) durometer squeegee

"Fat Bird," a two-color promotional T-shirt; another popular promotional object—the printed tote bag (inset)

A fashion T-shirt with a stylized floral motif. Printing manipulation makes this a one-of-a-kind T-shirt.

Among the plethora of printed T-shirts available, most fall within these three categories: promotional, commemorative, and designer/personalized.

- **Promotional T-shirts are used by advertisers to communicate to the consumer who will buy their products or services or adhere to their philosophy or ideas. In most cases, promotional T-shirts are given free to the public by the advertiser to increase demand or create goodwill.**

- **Commemorative T-shirts are printed to celebrate an event such as a festival, concert, or birthday. They can also be used as souvenirs to document a visit to a museum, monument, or city.**

- **Designer/personalized T-shirts are printed for the sole purpose of making a visual statement. They are used for adornment and for declaring one's personal style and individuality. Often one-of-a-kind, they are created by printing alone or by combining screen printing and other decorating techniques such as hand painting, tie dyeing, and collage or sewing.**

Pinning down and preparing a T-shirt for printing

PREPARING A T-SHIRT FOR PRINTING

1. **Stretch and pin down the shirt so that it doesn't move while printing, flattening the seams as much as possible (a).**

2. **Place a piece of thin plywood inside the shirt to prevent the ink from bleeding through. Cut it slightly larger than the shirt and spray it with adhesive so the ink will be blocked and the shirt will stay in place during printing. If plywood is not available, a thick layer of newspaper can also be used.**

Choosing a T-Shirt Design

When designing a T-shirt, it's best to use an eye-catching image that will capture a viewer's attention, such as one produced with unusual colors or printing techniques. It is not advisable to use designs with very fine lines or dots, since the knitted surface of a T-shirt combined with the required number of printing passes (at least four) may result in a loss of detail. A few other tips to remember:

- **Printing is usually done from the lightest of the colors to the darkest and from the least amount of ink to the most.**

- **If a third color is to be achieved by layering colors, the darker of the two is printed first, then the lighter.**

- **If you are printing opaque ink on a dark T-shirt and want more ink to go through without changing the mesh, use a softer squeegee (50 durometer). Soft squeegees allow more ink to go through the mesh and onto the substrate.**

- **When printing on the front of a shirt, the print should be positioned about 4" to 5" (10–12.5 cm) from the neckline. This is more of a suggested guideline than a hard-and-fast rule.**

The Engineered Print

An engineered print is a complete unit of a design meant to be printed on an object such as a decorative pillowcase, a place mat, a bag, or a scarf before the object is assembled by sewing. An engineered print is a "spot" print, not a repeat design, and it covers the whole area to be printed. It allows a design to have complete borders, perfect and elaborate corners, and bold solid stripes because all of the printing is done on one screen in the desired size.

In the case of a T-shirt where a typical front-printed logo is not sufficient, the engineered print is the way to go because it allows perfect printing near seams, buttons, pockets, collars, sleeves, and other parts of a garment—something that is rather difficult to do when the garment is sewn before printing. To achieve a fully decorated garment with printed images throughout, you can either print individual pattern pieces before sewing or print an entire length of fabric and then cut out the pattern accordingly.

Scarf printed in two different colorways

Another example of combining various designs to create a one-of-a-kind accessory, this 36" (91 cm) square scarf was made by combining three different screens. A screen with a simple texture design was printed first, then the one-color repeat of the leaves was added, followed by the image of the small tree. The border was done by hand using masking tape and a brush.

This 36" (91 cm) one-color, square scarf is printed by using a small screen containing one quarter of the image. It is printed four times in rotation to create the final design.

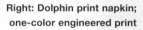
Dolphin place mat and napkin

Right: Dolphin print napkin;
one-color engineered print

Above: A one-color place mat and napkin engineered print. The screen was done photographically with actual lace as a positive.

A two-color design printed on a white cotton top, featuring a large Byzantine earring and a pair of stylized birds. The image was printed four times.

One-color engineered print on woven fabric. This print could easily be made into a decorative pillow.

Printing a simple engineered variation of an envelope bag. Designs can be recycled and screens can be combined with other screens to serve various needs and to create coordinates.

By changing inks and substrates, as well as adding backgrounds prior to printing, variations of a design can easily be achieved to serve a variety of purposes.

This finished envelope bag can be used by itself or with the "New York, New York!" commemorative T-shirt.

The Drama of Black and White

A black and white tote bag with a numbered print. The numbers are printed on pieces of white canvas that have been stitched together to make the bag.

When it comes to color, there is no "good" or "bad." What makes colors look beautiful or ugly, gaudy or sophisticated is the way they are combined. The combination of neutral tones such as black and white is known as achromatic (no color) harmony. And though black and white are technically colorless, the truth is there's nothing more dramatic and sophisticated than white pigment printed on a black substrate, or vice versa.

MATERIALS

- ▦ black or other dark-color substrate
- ▦ white opaque paint
- ▦ different color paints
- ▦ a screen with 110 (10xx) mesh with a design ready to be printed

A one-color design printed with black paint on a white T-shirt

A black-and-white photograph of a tree in winter inspired this repeat design. The tree design was combined with two other screen designs to create this interesting piece of fabric.

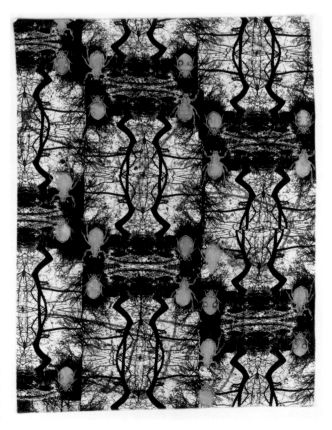

Once a screen is made, it can be printed on a variety of substrates and with a variety of inks. This leather print was produced with opaque textile inks and then made into a stylized belt. For permanence, the inks were sprayed with a fixative after printing.

So far we have worked with transparent inks that can achieve vivid depth of color, luminosity, and various other effects but that do very poorly when printed on black or other dark-colored substrates. The solution to this problem is opaque ink, which is ideal for printing on dark substrates using the following techniques:

1. Add white opaque to existing transparent paints. The more white added, the more opaque the paint becomes, producing a tint of the original color. It is therefore impossible to print red with this method because the red, by adding white, becomes pink.

2. Buy and print with ready-mixed opaque paints for textiles. They come in many opaque colors and become washable when properly heat-set, or cured, as is the case with all the paints used throughout these projects.

3. Yet another method for printing on dark substrates is "flash" printing, which follows these steps:

    -   Pin or glue the substrate on the printing table in a way that it keeps it from moving under the screen during printing.

    -   Place the screen over the substrate and mark the registration lines. You want to be sure you can go back to the same spot for a second time.

    -   Print first with opaque white (a).

    -   White opaque is thicker than transparent paints and is gluey; therefore, it requires more passes to go through the mesh. Also, it dries faster so the screen must not be left unattended for too long or the image areas will clog up. When "flash" printing, first print with opaque white.

    -   After the white is printed, clean the screen and let it dry. Let the print dry without moving it.

    -   Place the screen in the same position over the white print, and this time, introduce any transparent paint. Bright yellows, reds, and greens can be printed on black fabric with this method because the layer of white covers the ground color of the fabric and stops it from influencing the transparent paint (see b, page 75).

    -   When printing one layer of paint on another, you should add extra binder to the second layer of paint for better adhesion.

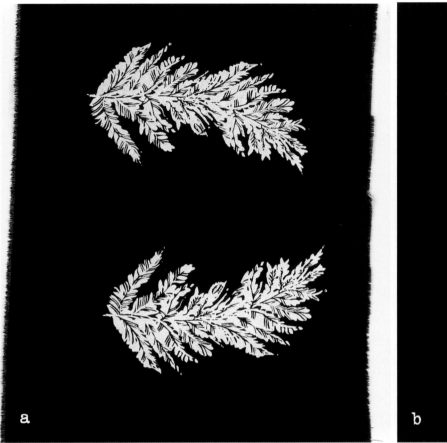

a

b

When "flash" printing, first print with opaque white.

The second step of "flash" printing using the rainbow printing technique (see page 47).

PLASTISOL INKS

For brilliant yellows, reds, purples, and greens on dark T-shirts and other fabric items, use plastisol inks. Because plastisol inks are oil-based and require mineral spirits for cleanup, they should only be used in a space with very good ventilation. Super opaque and somewhat plastic-like when dry, they come in a wide array of colors but cannot be air-dried. Prints made with plastisol inks require heat (about 300°F, or 150°C) for drying and fusion with the fiber of the substrate. After a printed garment is cured with heat, it becomes washable. Dry cleaning is not recommended.

This shows transparent inks, in this case blue, yellow, and red, printed directly onto black fabric.

Printing with Special Inks

PUFF PAINT

Puff paint looks and prints just like any other ink, until it dries. When it is heated the chemical composition reacts and puffs up, becoming three-dimensional. Any design can be printed using puff paint ink. However, it is not recommended for designs that have very large areas of print because it causes the fabric to buckle. In a multicolor design, only one or two of the colors should be printed with puff paint, leaving the rest in regular paint. This mixing creates an interesting print.

PHOSPHORESCENT INK

This ink glows in the dark after it has been exposed to light for 5–10 minutes. The glow eventually diminishes, but it can be regenerated over and over again by exposing the print to light.

METALLIC INK

Available in silver, gold, copper, and other metallic tones, these inks can be printed on fabric, paper, and many other substrates. They can be used as is or tinted with other water-based pigments for a vari-

ety of shades. However, if too much pigment (more than 3 percent) is added, they begin to lose their metallic look. Metallic inks are thicker than regular inks and require a lower count (6xx–8xx multifilament) mesh screen. Like puff paint and opaque inks, they also dry very quickly. (This process can be slowed down by adding a retarding catalyst like glycerine to the paint.)

GLITTER

Glitter is made from particles of polyester, and it can be used for decorating a screen-printed surface in two different ways. In the first method, the particles are dispersed in the glitter medium, which is printed on the substrate just like any other ink using a very course (16T or 25T) mesh. In the second method, a glitter adhesive is printed on the substrate through a 50–60T mesh, and then, while the adhesive is still wet, the glitter is sprinkled on and lightly padded onto the substrate, leaving the excess particles to be brushed off.

A piece of fabric with two designs printed with puff paint; one side is heat cured.

Metallic inks are almost always opaque or semi-opaque. This is a one-color screen printed with gold metallic ink in repeat on purple fabric with a texture previously printed on it.

You can achieve a brilliant look by using metallic powders (sold by the pound) and mixing them with the appropriate binder. For this water-based binder, you'd blend 2 pounds (0.9 kg) of powder to 1 gallon (3.8 L) of binder. Mix well and print with a medium squeegee and a screen with 4xx or 8xx mesh. After drying, the print must be cured at 300°F (150°C) to become washable.

Glitter printed on velvet and then made into pillows. For this print the glitter was mixed with its base and printed with a soft squeegee. The mesh of the screen was very coarse (16T), and the stencil was created photographically.

Discharge Printing: The Inkless Printing Technique

A collection of discharge prints on fabric

Discharge (or extract) printing uses bleaching chemicals like sodium formaldehyde sulphoxylate (SFS) to remove color from a fabric that has been dyed. Those areas become white and an image can then be printed within them in any color, creating a look that's similar to a blotch print.

MATERIALS

- a screen with a one-color image done in any technique
- black or other dark color T-shirts and fabrics
- a soft (50–60 durometer) round squeegee
- 1 quart (0.9 L) of Soft Scrub, Cif cream with bleach, or a discharge paste from an art supply store
- pair of gloves

A collection of prints on various substrates including a discharge print on black fabric.

Definition and Procedure

The chemical used to remove the dye for discharge printing depends on the kind of dye used. For a home studio, the safest discharge agent or chemical is chlorine bleach, which comes in paste form in the commonly used cleaning product Soft Scrub. The paste goes through 110 mesh with no problem. However, because it contains bleach, it must not be left on the screen for an extended period or it will destroy the emulsion. As soon as you're done printing, wash the screen to avoid over-bleaching. As a safety precaution, never mix bleach or Soft Scrub with ammonia or paint.

A discharge paste can be purchased at an art supply store and used on dark T-shirts instead of Soft Scrub. In either case, discharge printing should be done in a well-ventilated area and with the outmost care.

To use the discharge printing method, follow these steps:

1. Prepare the screen for printing and pin down the T-shirt or fabric to be printed, protecting it first by placing a piece of newspaper inside.

2. Most color T-shirts react to bleach. If you are printing on a dark fabric, test to see if it reacts by placing a drop of bleach at the corner. Wait at least 30 minutes and if no color has been removed then you know the fabric is not reacting to bleach and it cannot be used for this technique.

3. Place the screen on the substrate, and instead of ink, place a good amount of Soft Scrub in the inkwell space of the screen.

4. Print as you would with paint, allowing at least four to six passes for the Soft Scrub to saturate the substrate. For a double-face print, pass several more times until the Soft Scrub shows on both sides.

5. Wash the screen immediately after printing. Let the print air-dry and allow the bleach to work its way into the fiber. It might take an hour (or longer) before this happens.

6. After drying, wash the substrate with soap and water, removing all the bleach from the fiber so it does not destroy it.

Making a Photographic Screen with Textures

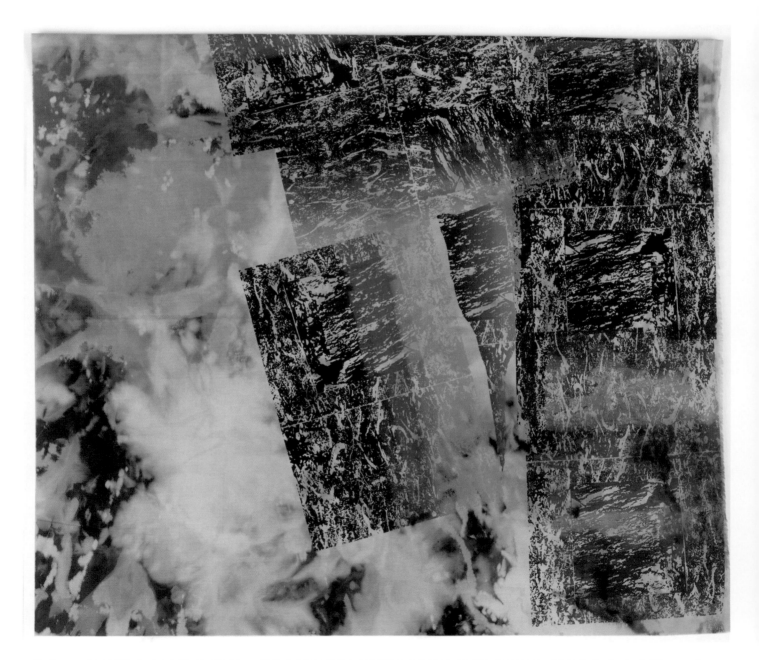

Texture screen printed on previously discharged black fabric. It is a good idea to keep a couple of screens with textures in stock. They can be used as backgrounds for other designs or as "fillers" when the need arises.

exture is one of the five basic elements of design, and the most subtle of all. It refers to how an object feels when touched, or, if it is an image of a texture, it suggests how it might feel when touched. Printed textures can easily simulate surfaces such as wood or leather and fabric constructions such as weaving, knitting, netting, or lace.

MATERIALS

- a photo emulsion sensitized screen with 110 mesh
- an empty screen and simple resist materials
- a positive with a textural image
- clear tape
- inks for printing texture, canning, and screenless printing techniques
- 2 or 3 various sizes of cans, opened on both ends
- about a pint of clear base or extender and a couple of (1" to 3") large brushes
- fabrics in dark colors that react to bleach and white for dyeing
- strings or rubber bands to tie fabric
- a 1 gallon (3.8 L) bucket
- liquid silk dyes (such as TinFix, Jacquard, or Dupont)
- cold water
- 1 quart (0.9 L) of bleach
- pair of gloves

A multicolored texture printed fabric. INSET: The same fabric embellished with opaque stars.

What Is Texture?

In textiles as well as other substrates, a texture might already exist in its construction and so should be taken into consideration when printing. Texture also affects the color of a surface, with smooth surfaces appearing shinier and brighter because they reflect the light better than rough materials do. When texture is desired as an overall design to change the look of the substrate or as a visual effect in only parts of a design, it can be added by printing.

A textural screen can be made by using the direct block out technique (pages 34–35) or it can be made photographically (page 44). A positive for a textural screen can be produced in various ways, including rubbing a texture onto acetate or vellum using a lithographer's crayon (or opaque China marker). You can also enlarge (by photocopying or scanning) a photograph of a textured object, such as the bark of a tree or the surface of a stone, or apply a texture onto acetate using opaque ink and a brush, sponge, or other textured material. Loosely woven fabrics and textural found objects like strings can be photographed directly onto a screen, just as long as the exposure time is reduced so the fine details don't burn out during exposure.

Altering the Substrate

There are a variety of ways to manipulate the substrate prior to printing, making it a more interesting surface to work with while still allowing the main design to take center stage. Techniques include:

RANDOMLY PRINTED COLOR PATCHES

This is a variation of the simple resist technique, and it can be used by itself or in combination with the texture screen. Basically, it allows shapes of color to be printed on the substrate via an empty screen, and it can be repeated several times with different shapes and colors.

CANNING (OR TIN CAN PRINTING)

For this technique the fabric is pinned down on the printing table very tightly, with the pins covered in packing tape all the way around. Using a tin can that has been opened on both ends, place it off the edge of the fabric near the tape. Press the can down, fill with paint, and pull to the other end of the fabric while pressing down.

You may go in a straight line and create a stripe, or you can zigzag or even make a circle. During canning, keep the pressure on the can consistent or the paint will escape and leave a blob on the substrate. When you're done, remove the can from the printing area by quickly pulling it onto a piece of cardboard.

Canning (or tin can printing) is an easy method for striping the substrate prior to printing a design.

SCREENLESS PRINTING

This technique is similar to canning, but instead of a tin can you use a sharp metal squeegee or the sides of a scoop coater. Prepare the substrate as above, placing the

During canning or screenless printing, resist areas can be drawn directly onto the substrate by applying a clear base or extender.

The colorful results of screenless printing

paint directly onto the tape at the top of the fabric. Create resist areas on the fabric (areas that maintain the color of the substrate) by applying an extender solution. While the extender is still wet, pull the squeegee and print, as if the fabric were a screen.

TIE-DYEING

Tie-dyeing, a resist technique in which selective areas are protected from receiving color, is one of the oldest methods for decorating fabric. It's achieved by tightly binding fabric with string or rubber bands prior to dipping it in a dye bath. The bound areas retain the original color of the substrate, creating an intricate pattern of circles, lines and shapes that varies based on the way the fabric is folded, knotted, or bound. The process can be very complicated and time-consuming, so it's up to the individual to decide how much effort to devote to it. Generally, the dyeing is done from the lightest to the darkest of the colors.

TIE-DISCHARGING

The reverse of tie-dyeing, this technique calls for removing color from sections of fabric by using bleach. After binding the material with string or rubber bands, dip it into an equal solution of bleach and cold water, allowing it to soak until the desired result is obtained. Once the discharge is complete, remove the fabric from the bath and rinse it immediately to stop the action of the bleach. Otherwise it might destroy the fiber of the fabric.

Tie-dyeing can produce a beautiful substrate that looks stunning when printed. The original fabric was white.

Samples of the tie-discharge technique. From the left, the original fabrics were blue, black, and dark green.

What About Paper?

An interesting serigraph has a cicada as subject matter.

Paper is an ideal surface for home screen printing because it absorbs water just as well as fabric, allowing full compatibility with water-based inks. Many artists create serigraphs (or screen prints on paper) for use as limited edition prints, posters, or cards. Although any paper is appropriate for screen printing, better results are achieved on papers with a smooth finish and compact size.

MATERIALS

- a screen with a 200 monofilament mesh
- a one-color design to be printed on paper
- several sheets of paper for printing
- an adhesive spray or double-sided tape
- water-based poster inks
- a hard (70-80 durometer) squeegee with a bevel edge profile
- four small pieces (about 1"x 1" [2.5 x 2.5 cm]) per screen of cardboard
- masking tape

Creating a space between the mesh and the substrate prevents the ink from spreading.

Marking the corners allows for accurate placement of the paper.

Lifting the screen off the printing area, flood the design with a thin layer of ink. Using a smooth stroke to push the ink away from you, hold the squeegee at a slight angle.

Print by pulling the squeegee toward you, forcing the thin layer of ink through the mesh.

CHOOSING THE PROPER INK

Although textile inks can be printed on some types of paper with good results, poster inks are ideal for paper because they're thicker in consistency and dry very quickly.

They can also be made transparent by adding an extender base and will produce a brilliant palette when blended.

Another option for printing on paper is permanent acrylic ink. This water-based paint is very similar to poster ink, but it dries waterproof on paper and can be used on a variety of substrates such as wood, Plexiglas, and even mirrors.

PRINTING ON PAPER

1. Prepare screen for printing as described on page 26. In addition, turn the screen printing side up and tape cardboard at the corners of the screen and on the mesh with masking tape. Creating a space between the mesh and the substrate prevents the ink from spreading (a).

2. Lock the screen in position with the clamps. With a marker, mark the position of the clamps onto the frame and make any other markings necessary to be able to go back in the same spot for a multicolor design or any other manipulation of the print.

3. Spray the plywood with an adhesive, place the paper down and press it in place. Mark the corners of the paper with masking tape to allow for accurate placement of all the other pieces of paper (b).

4. Place a generous amount of ink in the screen, then lifting the screen off the printing area, flood the design with a thin layer of ink. Using a smooth stroke to push the ink away from you, hold the squeegee at a slight angle (c).

5. Lower the screen onto the paper. Print by pulling the squeegee toward you, forcing the thin layer of ink through the mesh. Unlike printing on fabric, it's not necessary to have extra ink in front of the squeegee when printing on paper. The printing must be done quickly or the thin layer of ink will dry in the mesh (d).

6. Lift the screen from the print, flood the screen with ink, set the kick leg so the screen stays securely off the printing area, then remove the print and put it aside to dry.

7. Insert new paper following the markings of the masking tape, release the kick leg, and repeat the process until all the papers are printed. If you want to create a multicolor version of the design, print the first color on each copy and then set aside to dry. After cleaning the screen, repeat the process with each color until the desired result is achieved.

Tip: When a design has large areas of color, printing will cause the paper to buckle because of the water content in the ink. "Buckling" makes registration of colors difficult. To avoid this, keep each print under a flat weight after each color run is dry. You can also choose a paper that's rated 100 lbs (270 gsm) or higher, since the heavier the paper the less likely it is to buckle.

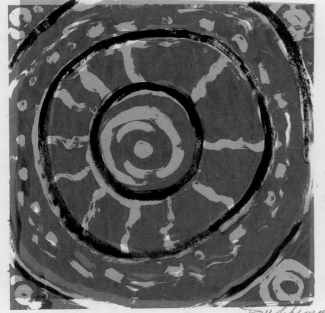

A serigraph done with the reduction printing technique that experiments with textile inks on paper: as a result the colors are softer and depth is achieved because of their transparency; the overall quality of the print is very painterly.

A simple one-color print on paper using blue water-based poster ink that employs the resist printing technique; the color is rich and even, resulting in the "true" look and quality of a serigraph.

Experimenting with Paper

The choice of papers is almost endless. Here are some terms you should know when shopping for supplies:

Calendering: The process used to give paper a smooth or glossy finish by pressing it between metal plates

Cold Pressed (CP): A paper with a medium surface achieved by pressing the paper between cold cylinders

Deckled: Paper with ragged edges

Hot Pressed (HP): Paper with a very smooth, glazed surface produced by pressing it between hot cylinders

Neutral pH (power of Hydrogen): If permanence of the serigraph is an important factor, then a paper with neutral pH (acid free) is important. Paper with excess acid will yellow and eventually deteriorate.

Ply: A single layer of paper. When several plies are bonded together, they form a board.

Rag: Paper made with non-wood fibers such as cotton or linen-pulp.

Rough: A grainy texture

Sizing: The addition of natural or synthetic materials to paper so as to control the amount of ink or paint it absorbs

Watermark: A design usually at the edge of the paper that is produced during the papermaking process, not by water but by raised wires on the mold

Weight: Gr: grams per square meter
Lbs: pounds per 500 sheets ream

OPPOSITE, TOP: "Expecting," a hand-painted serigraph. For a one-of-a-kind look, only the outline of the design is printed. The other colors were applied by hand with colored pencils.

OPPOSITE, BOTTOM: For this serigraph, a digitally produced positive was manipulated by scratching it with a craft knife. This haunting portrait of a young woman has four colors or screens.

A collection of screen-printed greeting cards

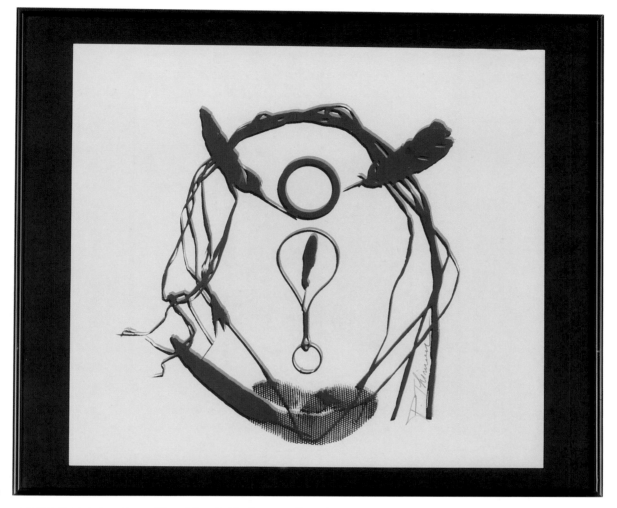

Serigraph on paper; composition of found objects suggesting a face

Where to Find Ideas and Inspiration

Always maintain a notebook with reference to colors and design ideas, as well as notes on tests runs, methods, and printing techniques.

Finding design ideas for screen printing is easy—just look around. The natural world provides inspiration in its fields and mountains, in the waters of its seas and rivers, and even in urban environments like city streets. The lines of cracked pavement, a mottled stone, or a beautifully textured tree trunk can all yield exciting designs. You can even enlarge and rearrange the skin of a cantaloupe to make a fascinating pattern, as shown in the image opposite at the right.

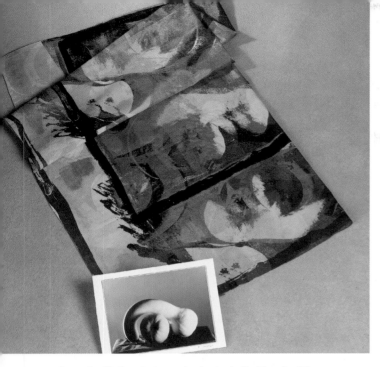

A scarf with the photograph of gourds that inspired it

Design ideas are plentiful when you pay attention. Even the skin of a cantaloupe can be used for its pattern.

The key is to become an observer. Every time you find a suggestive line or some attractive form or shape, jot down a quick note or sketch. Before long you'll have an entire notebook filled with ideas, each inspiring a printing project or an interesting chain of concepts to explore. When searching for design ideas, think:

- Architecture
- Asymmetry, abstract
- Balance, bands, borders
- Color, composition, cut-outs
- Dark and light
- Details
- Emphasis
- Function
- Geometric
- Grids
- Lines—fine, heavy, horizontal, vertical, diagonal, curved
- Landscapes
- Mass and movement
- Nature
- Optical, order
- Overall, originality
- Pattern, proportion
- Perspective
- Random, repeat, rectangular, round, rhythm,
- Silhouette, shape, scale, spiral, space, surface, structure, symmetry
- Symbol, still life
- Texture
- Unity
- Value, variety

IT'S ALL IN THE PRESENTATION

Once you have your ideas prepared, you should give plenty of thought to how you want your design to be presented. Presentation of any work is an art form and an important selling point, and basic elements such as neatness, unity, coherence, and clarity must always be addressed for good communication. It's also important to make a statement and illustrate a specific theme, which can be based on a shape in the design, a color, a purpose or function, or the quality of the substrate.

Once printing is complete, large pieces of fabric should be trimmed so no unprinted areas are visible. If you decide not to use the material for a garment or other accessory, you can mount it on a presentation board, with neatly folded edges taped to the back.

Paper prints should always be mounted and, if possible, appropriately framed. If a serigraph is not framed it should be protected by covering it with clear acetate or tracing paper. A combination of different prints on a variety of substrates can be displayed together in a way that creates a powerful visual statement.

Troubleshooting: Common Screen Print Problems and Their Solutions

PROBLEM: ARTWORK DOES NOT OPEN AFTER EXPOSURE AND DURING WASHING

Light goes through during exposure because the positive is not opaque enough, burning the image. Or, there is poor contact between the positive and the mesh of the screen.

Solutions:

- Use more weights to achieve good contact.

- If possible, make a copy of the artwork and double it. This will produce a more opaque positive.

- Reduce the exposure time. The screen may have fogged because it was left too long in the light.

PROBLEM: THE ARTWORK WASHES OFF WHILE DEVELOPING THE SCREEN (KNOWN AS WASHOUT BREAKDOWN)

Solutions:

- The screen is underexposed. Increase exposure time.

- Too much water pressure. Do not use hot water because it dissolves unexposed emulsion much faster than cold water. Emulsion is applied thickly onto the mesh. Press against the mesh as you apply the emulsion and use the sharpest of the edges on the scoop coater to get a thin, even layer of emulsion.

PROBLEM: HAZING OR SCUMMING

Solutions:

- The screen is underexposed and not washed properly. Some emulsion residue is interfering with having a sharp print. Sometimes this hazing disappears as the pressure of the squeegee opens up the areas.

- The light scattered during exposure, causing undercutting. This can be prevented by using a dyed mesh instead of white or by improving the contact between the positive and the mesh.

PROBLEM: THE PRINT HAS STRAIGHT LINES THAT LOOK LIKE A SAW (KNOWN AS SAW-TOOTH EDGE)

This occurs when there is too much water pressure and heat.

Solutions:

- Always use cold water after exposure and rinse gently.

- Make sure the mesh is evenly and completely coated and that it's properly stretched.

PROBLEM: EXCESSIVE PINHOLES ON THE SCREEN

Solutions:

- The emulsion is not completely dry prior to exposure. It appears to be dry but it is still wet underneath.

- Dust has blown onto the screen while wet. Dust the film, dry screen, or glass of the exposure unit.

- The screen is not coated properly. Coat it more than once, especially if it is a coarse mesh.

- The screen has been over washed. Repeat the exposure process, but do so more gently.

PROBLEM: THE PHOTO STENCIL BREAKS DOWN QUICKLY

Solutions:

- This happens when the screen is underexposed. Repeat the process, extending the exposure time.

- The emulsion is too thin and not thoroughly dry before exposure. Repeat the process, allowing the emulsion to fully dry.

- The mesh is not tightly stretched on the frame, and the loose stencil adds to the friction of the squeegee on the emulsion. Make sure the mesh is tightly stretched.

PROBLEM: THE PRINT WASHES OFF THE FABRIC

The problem is referred to as crocking and is caused by under-curing the print.

Solutions:

- To test for crocking before washing the print, use a clean white piece of cloth and rub it against the print. If everything is done, no ink should rub off. If it does, the print is not cured properly, or the ink is not mixed in the right proportions of vehicle and pigment. Add more binder to the ink and cure the print longer or at higher temperature.

Gallery

se these images as inspiration for your own screen-printed works of art. The variety of textures, tones, colors, and compositions offers something for everyone!

Artist: Paul Thimou

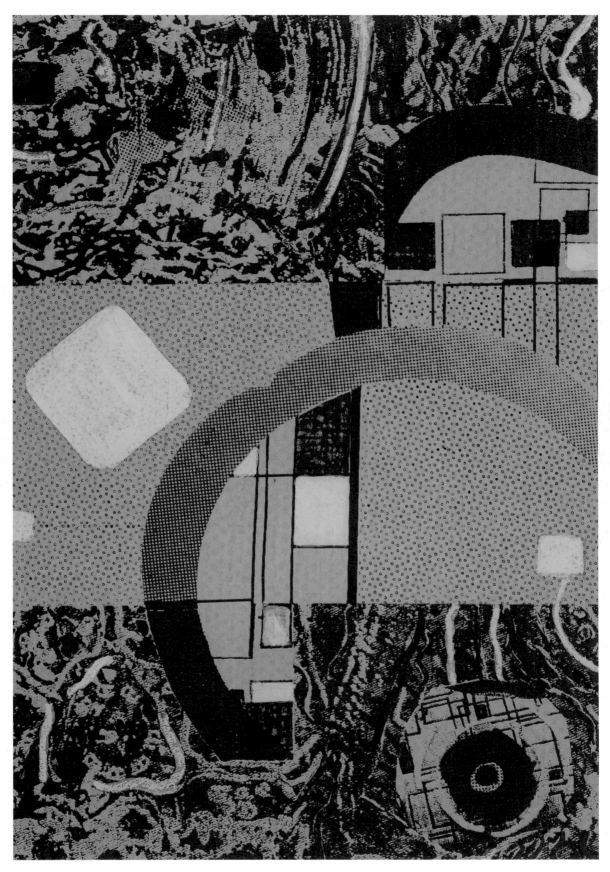

Artist: Paul Thimou

Artist: Paul Thimou

Artist: Paul Thimou

Artist: Paul Thimou

Artist: Paul Thimou

Artist: Paul Thimou

Artist: Paul Thimou

Artist: Paul Thimou

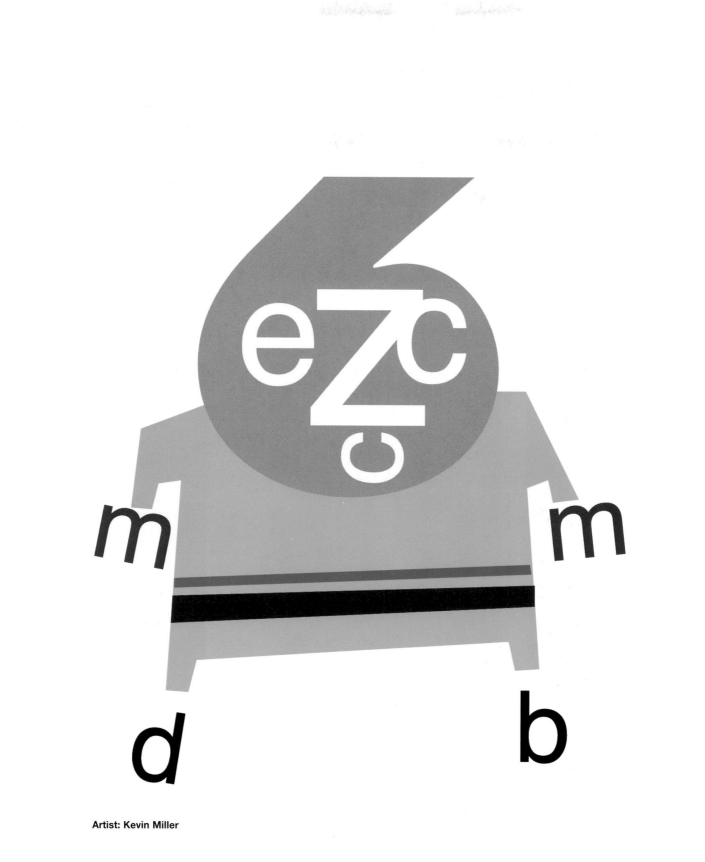

Artist: Kevin Miller

Artist: Isabelle Malouf (age 12)

Artist: Laura McFadden

Artist: Laura McFadden

Artist: Jenna Talbot

Artist: Laura McFadden

Artist: Laura McFadden

Artist: Laura McFadden

Artist: Kevin Miller

Artist: Laura McFadden

DIA DEL MUERTE

Artist: Laura McFadden

Artist: Laura McFadden

Artist: Paul Thimou

Artist: Paul Thimou

Artist: Paul Thimou

Glossary

Acetate: Clear or frosted and translucent plastic material upon which a design is painted, with an opaque medium, to produce a film positive for photographing a screen

Binder: Substance in which the colorants (pigments) are added to make a paste (ink) that can be printed. The binder contains the catalysts that make the pigments stick to the substrate.

Bleeding: Spreading of the color outside the printed areas as to give a shadow effect.

Block-out: The liquid used to draw a design directly onto the mesh of a screen. During printing, these areas do not print but remain negative in the color of the substrate.

Color Separation: Procedure used to break down a design to its individual color components. Positives are made of each color and into a screen. The design is then reassembled during printing.

Dots-per-inch (dpi): The measurement used to indicate how many dots appear within a square inch of a design. The number defines the quality of an image's resolution. A high number indicates high resolution, and a low, the opposite.

Durometer: Method of measuring the softness or hardness of a squeegee's blade

Direct Printing: A printing method where the color is printed directly onto the substrate

Discharge Printing: A printing technique during which a paste containing a bleaching agent is printed through a screen instead of pigment. The bleaching agent removes the dye from the fabric, forming the pattern of the design within the discharged areas.

Extender: Paste used to reduce the color value of the paint

Fastness: The ability of a color (pigment) to withstand washing and exposure to light without losing its chroma

Flooding: Covering the printing area in a screen with a thick layer of ink so that it does not clog waiting for the next print. Flooding the design first and then printing is done when the substrate cannot handle too much ink.

Ground Color: The original color of the fabric before printing on it

Halftones: Artwork made up by combining different sizes of dots and different spacing between them

Migration: Another term for when the color of a print is bleeding in negative areas

Moire: A distorting pattern created when two or more layers of geometric elements such as dots are placed one on top of the other at an incorrect angle

Monofilament: Mesh woven from a single continuous strand of manmade threads

Multifilament: Mesh woven from many manmade threads twisted to form a single strand

MSDS: Material Safety Data Sheet: Information about materials and their chemicals. The consumer needs to know the chemical composition of the materials being used to avoid hazardous situations, and the manufacturer is obliged by the law to supply this information.

Negative Space: The space around or between design elements in a composition. An area that is not printed but remains the color of the substrate.

Opacity: The quality of a surface to stop light from going through it

Overprinting: Printing one color over another

Photo Emulsion: Emulsion that becomes light sensitive after it dries and water insoluble after it is exposed to UV light. It is used to photograph images onto a screen.

Pigments: Substances that color the fiber of the fabric. Pigments sit on the surface of the substrate and do not penetrate the fiber.

Pinholes: Tiny holes in the emulsion area on the screen after it has being exposed and washed. If left uncovered they print as very fine dots.

Positive: Artwork ready to be transferred to a screen. It is done on a transparent or translucent base with an opaque medium. Eventually, opaque areas will print and clear areas will not.

Random Printing: The design unit is printed freely all over a piece of fabric several times until an irregular pattern is created.

Registration: During printing, exact alignment of one color to another in a multicolor design

Register Marks: Small markings (usually crosses) placed at the corners of a design and at straight lines. Register marks are needed to mark the screens so they all go precisely were they should when printing a multicolor design.

Repeat: The undetected flow and joint of one unit of design to the other when printed to produce a long piece of fabric.

Resist: Any material that adheres to the mesh of the screen or the substrate and prevents the ink from reaching designated areas of the substrate.

Retardant: A liquid that is added to a water-base paint to slow down its drying and prevent the mesh from clogging

Reduction Printing: Printing technique during which the design is overprinted several times, each time with a new color and progressively reduced printing area

Saw Tooth: The unwanted broken-up line of a print, which is the result of poorly coating the screen with emulsion

Scoop Coater: The metal tool used to apply emulsion to the mesh of the screen

Serigraph: A print (on paper) done for fine arts purposes by using the process of screen printing

Squeegee: A tool used during printing to push the paint through the mesh of the screen and onto the substrate. It's made out of a wooden handle and a rubber blade.

Stencil: Material such as paper or film from which areas have been selectively removed to create openings that will allow ink to go through and imprint a design on a surface

Substrate: Any material intended for printing

Screen Printing: Method of selectively decorating a surface. The color is forced onto the surface through a stencil made on a fine fabric that is stretched on a frame.

Tie-dye: Technique of dyeing fabric. The fabric is tied first in knots or other manners and then dipped into a dye-bath. The areas that are tied receive little or no color at all.

Trapping: In printing, an easy way of getting a third color by printing transparent color on color (darker first, lighter second); in color separation, a thin line created by printing color on color (light first, dark second) to help avoid a white gap between two colors

Resources

AA Screen Printing Supplier, Inc.
1087 S. Marietta Pkwy. S.E.
Marietta, GA 30060 USA
(800) 334-4513
www.aasps.com

Casey's Page Mill, Ltd.
For ink-jet and laser films for digital positives
6528 South Oneida Ct.
Englewood, CO 80111 USA
(800) 544-5620
www.caseyspm.com

LGN
P.O. Box 4970
Syracuse, NY 13221 USA
(888) 840-1371
www.systemfacilities.com

Nazdar
An international manufacturer and distributor of screen printing products
www.nazdar.com

The Specialty Graphic Imaging Association
Supporting the leaders of the digital and screen printing community
www.sgia.org

Speedball Art Products Company
2226 Speedball Rd.
Statesville, NC 28677 USA
(800) 898-7224
www.speedballart.com

Standard Screen Supply Corp.
121 Varick St.
New York, NY 10013 USA
(800) 221-2697
www.standardscreen.com

The Textile Society of America, Inc.
An international forum for the exchange and dissemination of information about textiles
www.textilesociety.org

Textile Industries Media Group
Textile news and general resources
www.textileworld.com

U.S. Screen Print Institute
Covering screen print and inkjet technology
www.usscreen.com

Union Ink
453 Broad Ave.
Ridgefield, NJ 07657 USA
(800) 526-0455
www.unionink.com

About the Author

Paul Thimou was introduced to the screen printing process in the early 1980s after studying photography at the New York Institute of Photography. He uses screen-printing techniques alone and in combination with other methods to produce artwork for exhibitions and crafts for selling or giving as gifts. He teaches at New York City's Fashion Institute of Technology.

Acknowledgments

I would like to thank all my students at the Textile/Surface Design Department of the Fashion Institute of Technology in New York City who through the years have inspired me, challenged me, and in general kept me on my toes. My thanks to Theodore Thimou for his invaluable help in writing this book. For her help in producing many of the samples, I would like to thank Ms. Luisa Padilla. For her support, inspiration, and friendship, I thank my teacher, friend, and colleague Zsuzsi Dahlquist. Finally, I thank my partner in experimentation and research, Carole Joseph.